SACRED
BULL

SACRED BULL

The Inner Obstacles
That Hold You Back at Work
and How to Overcome Them

ALBERT J. BERNSTEIN, PH.D.
SYDNEY CRAFT ROZEN

JOHN WILEY & SONS, INC.

New York • Chichester • Brisbane • Toronto • Singapore

Library of Congress Cataloging-in-Publication Data:

Bernstein, Albert J.
    Sacred bull : the inner obstacles that hold you back at work and
  how to overcome them / Albert J. Bernstein, Sydney Craft Rozen.
      p.   cm.
    ISBN 0-471-59836-4
    1. Psychology, Industrial.   2. Employees—Counseling of.
  3. Behavior modification.   I. Rozen, Sydney Craft.   II. Title.
  HF5548.8.B394   1994
  158.7—dc20   94-11920

Printed in the United States of America
10 9 8 7 6 5 4 3 2 1

To our children,
Jessica and Joshua Bernstein,
and Geoffrey and Amanda Rozen

and

To Lee,
for getting well again

PREFACE

This book is about the obstacles we place in front of ourselves, most of which we never realize or question.

To see what we mean, let's take a look at an all-too-typical work scene.

. . . It was supposed to have been a cooperative inter-departmental meeting. Unfortunately, it turned into the kind of group encounter you'd find in a Stephen King novel.

Anna from Engineering is always willing to waste everybody else's time on her obsession with every little detail. There's just one detail this perfectionist consistently overlooks: projects have deadlines.

Rick from Research and Development tries to convince everybody that he's the natural choice for project leader. The guy is so political that he needs a campaign manager. Look out for him. You can be sure he'll be looking out for himself.

If there were any fairness, you'd be named team leader.

Who else deserves it more? But you'd rather sit here in dignified silence than stoop to blowing your own horn.

The maneuvering goes on, and there's nobody to stop it—certainly not Harris, the VP sitting in for upper management. Harris is a conflict-avoider from the word maybe. *He always agrees completely with the last person he talks to. If his foot were on fire, he'd call headquarters for permission to put it out—and then wait for instructions.*

This is the same business bull you have to put up with every day. You probably work with people like this. They're competent and smart. They all believe they're doing the right thing. Yet their perfectionism, blatant self-interest, and avoidance of conflict are holding them back and blocking the progress of the group.

You can see *their* problems clearly. But do you recognize your own?

You may be blocking your own progress at work because of assumptions you've made about how people—yourself included—operate. You probably don't question or even think about these assumptions; you just let them mess up your job. Probably they're holding back your career advancement, preventing you from working effectively with bosses, colleagues, and subordinates, and limiting your ability to make effective decisions.

What if the ideas you accept without question are based on a lot of bull?

This book is about the inner obstacles you create for yourself at work. You build these obstacles from assumptions about how you and other people should act. Over time these assumptions become the rules by which you respond to people and situations. You may believe them without question and operate by them without thinking about the consequences. Even when they're wrong, you hold them sacred.

These unquestioned assumptions become your Sacred

Bulls. They cause you to make the same mistakes over and over by thinking things that *should* be true and doing things that *ought* to work.

In India, cows sacred to vengeful Hindu gods are allowed to roam wherever they choose. They can eat a person's lunch, block traffic, disrupt commerce, and generally stand in the way of India's becoming a modern, industrialized country.

The unruly beasts that block your progress don't have horns and tails. You can't see them. For the most part, you don't even think about them, much less recognize them as the sources of ineffectiveness at work. They are the rules you live by, beliefs that are incorrect but never questioned.

The ten Sacred Bulls that create obstacles to your progress at work are the Bulls of:

1. *Denial: I don't see the problem, so it isn't there.*
2. *Blind Spots and Shortcuts: What I don't like can't be important.*
3. *Self-Interest: Always look out for Number One.*
4. *Mind Reading: People should know what I want without being told.*
5. *Blame: If something goes wrong, it has to be somebody's fault.*
6. *Being Nice: Avoid conflict at all cost.*
7. *Perfection: If it's not perfect, it's nothing.*
8. *Fairness: I don't need to negotiate for what I want; I just want fairness.*
9. *Excuses: There's always a good reason why I don't follow the rules everyone else works by.*
10. *Being Right: There's a right way and a wrong way; my way is right.*

Sacred Bull: The Inner Obstacles That Hold You Back at Work and How to Overcome Them turns the focus of Dr. Albert Bernstein's twenty years of experience in psychotherapy and business consulting toward an examination of these unquestioned and frequently self-destructive beliefs. *Sacred Bull* goes below the surface and helps you look at and understand the obstacles that stand in your way.

What you do doesn't always get you the results you expect. When things go wrong, you may push harder, clamp down, or blame others. You may question everything around you—except the real source of the problem: your Sacred Bulls. This book helps you to rethink why you do what you do and offers ways to make changes toward becoming more effective, productive, and happy.

What are the obstacles you're creating for yourself at work?

Maybe, like Anna in the example, you're having problems with perfectionism. It's a vice that masquerades as a virtue. It makes you feel as if you're accomplishing a lot and generally doing the world a favor. But perfectionists tend to become obsessed with details and the need for control, and to forget about the big picture. Eventually this catches up with you, and you feel like a complete failure. Worse yet, your behavior is so annoying to other people that they will gladly make all the mistakes you so scrupulously avoid just to spite you.

Or, like Rick the office politician, maybe you've been focusing too much on looking out for Number One. Isn't that the basis of any successful career? If you believe that, you may be engaging in knee-jerk competition even when you could gain more by cooperating.

Or how about fairness? If you expect other people to treat you fairly, you're in for one disappointment after another when they don't. The bigger problem is that you never learn to negotiate for what you want, which ensures that you never get fair treatment.

Maybe you sympathize with Harris, the conflict-avoiding VP? You hate choosing sides and don't like to make other people angry at you. Often, to solve a problem, you have to be willing to take the Bull by the horns.

We're sure you know people who act like this. But do you recognize yourself? If not, you just might be following the Sacred Bull of Denial: "I don't see the problem, so it isn't there." This book will help you recognize and confront the obstacles that are holding you back.

ALBERT J. BERNSTEIN, PH.D.
SYDNEY CRAFT ROZEN

Portland, Oregon
Bothell, Washington
August 1994

ACKNOWLEDGMENTS

The authors thank:

John Mahaney, World's Greatest Editor, who produced more saves on this project than the entire New York Mets bullpen.

Elizabeth Wales, our agent, who fought the good fight for us from Oz, through the Swamp, all the way to the Bull.

Al thanks:

Luahna, Jessica, and Joshua, for their help, support, and love.

Mindy Ranik, for listening to a lot of these ideas before they were ideas.

Bill Casey, for his stimulating thoughts and unflagging empiricism.

Byron Griffin, for transcribing the random notes that became this manuscript.

Sydney thanks:

Lee, whose perfectionistic, blind-spotted, conflict-avoiding writer-wife could not have done this without you (and that's no Bull).

Geoff, whose loving, bottom-line encouragement kept your grateful mom focused. (The Miata has to be *red*.)

Amanda, whose sympathetic hugs and intelligent questions about the metaphor helped save the Sacred Bull.

Also, Norma Gunning, for a mother's heart and businesswoman's savvy; Lora Pellegrini, for wise advice to keep *la porta aperta*; Elmer Pellegrini, for upbeat courage; Bill Rozen, for Wednesday night pep-talks-by-phone; and Ken Gunning, for the Motown-and-blues tape that made me want to sing, even while proofreading the Bull.

A.J.B.
S.C.R.

CONTENTS

don't like to do, especially in our dealings with other people. The truth is, the hard way *is* the easy way. That's not what the Bulls want you to think.

CHAPTER FOUR
THE BULL OF SELF-INTEREST: Look Out for Number One 63

It's easy to dress up the Law of the Jungle to look like up-to-the-minute management theory—especially when you're the biggest predator in the jungle. This Bull causes people to choose reflex competition over cooperation every time. If you trust people, you get eaten. It's the law.

CHAPTER FIVE
THE BULL OF MIND READING: People Should Know Without Being Told 91

It feels so good to believe that if people have the right feelings on the inside, they will do the right things on the outside. Of course, this belief feels so good because it completely absolves you of any responsibility to ask for what you want—or of any responsibility to manage people. Relying on mind reading requires your employees to manage *you*, rather than vice versa.

CHAPTER SIX
THE BULL OF BLAME: It Has to Be Somebody's Fault 113

When something goes wrong, it's so emotionally satisfying to fix the blame. Who cares that fixing blame does nothing to fix the problem?

CHAPTER SEVEN
THE "NICE" BULL: Avoid Conflict at All Cost 133

Telling people what they want to hear instead of the truth is often tempting. You avoid little altercations in the present by setting yourself up for bigger ones in the future.

CHAPTER EIGHT
THE BULL OF PERFECTION: If It's Not Perfect, It's Nothing 156

Perfectionism is a vice that often masquerades as a virtue. It's hard to estimate how many problems one perfectionist can create. People make more mistakes when they are around someone whose impossible demands frighten them or make them angry.

CHAPTER NINE
THE BULL OF FAIRNESS: I Don't Need to Negotiate for What I Want—I Just Want Fairness! 179

Saying "I just want fairness" is much more socially acceptable than saying "If I don't get mine first, I don't play." Both versions, however, mean the same thing. Fairness is a useful concept for thinking about how to treat other people. When you use it to think about how others should treat you, it's merely the opening shot in a lifelong battle.

CHAPTER TEN
THE BULL OF EXCUSES: There's a Good Reason! 202

Some people "spin-doctor" themselves by believing their own excuses. It's harder but far more rewarding to face reality and do what you have to do to get results. The road to hell is paved with good intentions. This Bull holds the paving contract.

CHAPTER ELEVEN
THE "RIGHT" BULL: There's a Right Way and a Wrong Way—My Way Is Right 230

Life often offers a cruel choice. You can be right or you can be effective. People who would rather be right seldom get to be either. Thinking that being reasonable means doing it your way is a prescription for inefficiency and resentment.

Sacred Bulls can rob you of the things that make your job feel it's worth doing. Now that you recognize them for what they are, here's how to get them out of your life for good.

Chapter One

WATCH OUT FOR THE BULL

A llen's eyes snapped open. The digital clock said 3 A.M.
He clamped his eyes shut and willed himself to relax
and get some sleep. He would need to be sharp and alert
for his meeting tomorrow with Dalton, "the Enforcer." The
senior VP for finance was coming all the way out here
from headquarters to talk to Allen about his division. The
Enforcer rarely "talked," he passed sentences.

Allen stared up through the darkness at the bedroom
ceiling, wondering how things had gotten so out of control.
The problems had started three years ago, when he was
transferred from the Finance Department at headquarters
to this division. He thought his new assignment would be
a snap. He'd always believed that managers in the field
didn't have the financial savvy to do things right. He was
all set to show up the other divisions and go back to headquarters, covered with glory.

The division he was sent to manage was doing okay—
just okay—in production, sales, and customer service. This
was no shining star. Allen knew costs were running on the

1

high side, but he had promised, sight unseen, that he could improve the profit picture. How hard could it be? He had never seen an operation yet that couldn't be cut a few percentage points.

Allen prided himself on his years of accounting experience. He was a real perfectionist where waste was concerned. What he hadn't counted on were the impossible people he'd have to work with, people who managed to torpedo everything he was trying to do.

The transfer had been his big chance. If he could get control of this division and show some impressive numbers, he'd have a shot at a VP seat at headquarters. Now that chance was sinking, along with his hopes for the rest of his career.

"What We Do Know That Ain't So"

If there's one thing you learn in twenty years of practice in business consultation and psychotherapy, it's that people don't always know what they're doing. (No offense, Allen.) What we do doesn't always get us the results we expect. Sometimes what we do doesn't square with what we say we believe. We all have enormous capacity to hide these facts from ourselves.

It was Allen's own mistaken beliefs about how things should be done, not his subordinates, that fired the torpedo. Allen assumed that if he managed the money, everything else would take care of itself. It did, but not in the way he expected.

When things go wrong, we may push harder, clamp down, or blame others, but few of us ever question the basic beliefs by which we operate. As we manage our careers and our life at work, we seldom ask ourselves, "What am I really trying to accomplish here? Is this the best way to get it done?" We just continue with more of the same and wonder why the situation grows steadily worse. The result is that we feel trapped, bogged down, and overwhelmed.

In this book we identify and explain, with many examples, the ten most common mistaken assumptions about human behavior. We call these beliefs Sacred Bull.

How Allen Torpedoed Himself

Let's look in again on Allen, sleepless from the cold fear that he is going to be fired.

Allen shifted restlessly on his pillow, remembering. On his second day here, he had announced The Audit. He realized now that it had probably been a mistake to do it so soon, but he'd needed to show everyone that he held the reins of power in a firm grip. Maybe he should have developed a better rapport with the staff first, but that touchy-feely stuff was never his strong suit. Give him the numbers any day. Allen shut his eyes. He just hoped the Enforcer wasn't coming to tell him his *number was up.*

Allen had met with each department head and demanded a detailed balance sheet and justification for every expenditure. He wanted his managers to start thinking carefully about each dollar they spent. What he wanted to hear was how they could make things more efficient.

A couple of them got it. Allen had been relieved to see that he'd inherited a little decent management material along with the deadwood. Most of the department heads had missed the point, though. They'd waltzed in, all eager smiles and earnest speeches about how great their departments were and how their teams could be even better by using more resources. He was shocked at their naiveté.

Jana, for instance, kept asking for more clerical support for her sales reps. Maybe more help would *have made them more productive, but why couldn't she figure out that the*

3

company frowned on adding new positions in this economic climate? With the start-up time, plus the training, salaries, and benefits, the profit picture would have looked bad for an entire quarter.

And what made her think it was clerical help, rather than hard work and responsible management, that would lead to more sales? Spending more doesn't automatically improve performance. Allen shouldn't have had to explain this to Jana. He had understood when he was at her level. Nobody had told him what was expected. He just knew. Didn't everybody "just know"? (At least, everybody who's any good.)

Then there was Richard and all his ideas about customer surveys and follow-up. Allen snorted. Richard had obviously let this total quality management stuff addle his brain. He should have been keeping the motivation high in his own department. Why ask questions? If people were buying the product, they liked it. Instead of spending money on customer surveys that might demotivate his sales force, Richard should have been pumping up his team to make more contacts and push the high-profit items.

Allen didn't dislike Richard. He had seen in him the idealism of his own youth. But Richard needed to learn some hard lessons, then maybe he'd shape up and be a decent manager. Allen had expected more of him than some of the others. He'd tried to shake him up a little, pushed him hard to get the best out of him, just as some of Allen's bosses had pushed him. He had hated them for it at the time but thanked them later on. He'd expected the same response from Richard. Instead, Richard had broken under the pressure.

Allen had seen in the first week that most of his managers just didn't understand how the game was played. He kept telling them, but they didn't get it. Sure, he believed in good customer service and TQM, but fiscal responsibility always comes first. His managers didn't have their priorities straight. It hadn't taken him long to figure out that the *division was out of control and everybody needed a crash course in how things were really done.*

ALLEN'S UNQUESTIONED BELIEFS

If you asked Allen what had caused his problems, he would probably complain of naive managers, a poor work ethic in the division, and tight economic times. What he would not tell you is that *he* had created a fair number of his problems himself.

Of course, he wasn't intending to do that. Allen's agenda was to get his division running as smoothly and efficiently as possible. He did this by instituting tight financial controls, assuming that if he controlled the money, people would control themselves. He never gave a thought to how to approach his managers to get the results he wanted. He didn't see that another approach would make any difference. Tell people what to do and they do it, right? Allen believed that his approach to management was perfectly logical. Everybody else made it needlessly complicated.

Every manager had left Allen's office that first week with a mission: Cut at least 5 percent from his or her operation. Allen knew it would be almost impossible for some, but he wanted them all thinking about cutting costs rather than about spending money.

He decided that the best way to do this was to use the natural competitive urge and good old self-interest as motivators. He had offered a percentage of what they cut above 5 percent as a bonus to managers, and he strongly suggested that the people who didn't make the 5 percent goal might have to look for jobs elsewhere. One thing he knew about psychology: If you allow people to stay in their comfort zones, they get careless and lazy. No way would he let that happen in his division.

Some of the managers had handled the heat very well. Others handled the challenge with finger pointing, bickering over the smallest expenditure, and complaining to him about "group cohesion" falling apart. There was shouting about participating in management decisions and other fear-related behavior that Allen expected. Looking back, though, he saw that things had fallen apart far worse than he'd anticipated.

Jana resigned because she felt Allen was being "unfair." Yeah, right. Losing anyone who believes business is fair is good riddance. He had given the department to one of her juniors, who had big plans for meeting Allen's target figures. He did, too. The kid cut costs and moved product. It had taken about a year for the turnover rate and the dissatisfied customers to show up on the bottom line.

Allen sighed. The guy's heart had been in the right place, but Allen hadn't intended for him to cut so many corners. He had had to get rid of him and step in to run the department himself to clean up the mess. Well, you know what they always say: If you want it done right, do it yourself.

Of course, by then Allen was spread pretty thin, too thin to really check out the numbers from the other departments—especially Richard's. Richard had turned into an expert at telling Allen what he wanted to hear. But there had been a lot going on in that department that Allen hadn't known about. Richard just couldn't bring himself to tell him. What a disappointment he'd turned out to be.

Allen was just getting things under control again with a few management changes (Richard couldn't stand the heat) when the call had come from Dalton. Great. How could headquarters expect him to have foreseen the kind of attitude problems and naiveté he'd walked into? Now, just when he was getting things under control, it looked as if he was going to lose his job because of the incompetence and inexperience of people like Jana and Richard.

Allen had a sinking feeling that the Enforcer wouldn't

give him the chance to explain how the division was start-ing to turn around. He fumbled for his glasses and turned on the bedside lamp. There was no way he'd be able to get back to sleep before dawn. Might as well do something productive. He reached for the spreadsheets on the nightstand.

Allen thought he knew how to play the corporate game. He actually knew very little about how people, including himself, actually operate. He had been running his division by a set of destructive but unquestioned beliefs. He genuinely believed he was doing what was best for his division and could not understand why he kept getting negative results. He did not see the Sacred Bulls that were causing the problems.

THE TEN SACRED BULLS

The ten Sacred Bulls are the beliefs you follow without thinking. They are the ideas that nobody checks or ques-tions because "We've always done it this way." Everybody "knows" they're true. These beliefs actually stand square in the way of common sense. They are the source of many of your frustrations at work.

The following are the ten Sacred Bulls:

1. Denial: I Don't See It, So It Isn't There

Allen practiced denial each time he listened to Jana and Richard complain about how he was running the depart-ment. Rather than seeing their objections as indications of a real problem he needed to deal with, Allen dismissed what they said as evidence of bad attitudes and lack of experience.

2. Blind Spots and Shortcuts: What I Don't Like Can't Be Important

Allen's blind spot was numbers: everything that wasn't fiscal wasn't worth worrying about. To him, getting good performance from his department was all a matter of numbers—the area he understood best. Subtleties, such as how he pressured Richard and Jana into acting the way they did, were lost on him.

3. Self-Interest: Look Out for Number One

Allen felt he could get the most out of his managers by putting them in competition with each other. He had always believed that competition would bring out the best in people. Instead, in his department it led to distrust and a sense among his managers that they were adversaries to be subdued rather than team members to be heeded.

4. Mind Reading: People Should Know Without Being Told

Allen rewarded the people who saw the department the same way he did. If they saw things any other way, he believed they just didn't have the right stuff on the inside.

5. Blame: It Has to Be Somebody's Fault

Allen saw his career as torpedoed by inept managers. He never saw his own finger on the firing button. Much of what his managers did was actually in response to Allen's behavior. (They didn't think they had any other choice.) Getting rid of Richard and Jana did nothing to help Allen's career, but blaming and punishing them seemed like the right thing to do at the time.

6. Being Nice: Avoid Conflict at All Cost

Richard discovered that, as unpleasant as conflict may be, it's nothing compared with what happens when you try to avoid conflict. Allen's program to shape him up felt like one criticism after another. Eventually Richard grew so sick of the conflict that he simply told Allen whatever he thought Allen wanted to hear. When the facts caught up with him, there was no place for Richard to go but out.

7. Perfection: If It's Not Perfect, It's Nothing

Perfectionism is a vice that masquerades as a virtue. It's difficult to estimate how many problems one perfectionist can create. For a rough estimate, just look at Allen's department. Allen's relentless demands more often caused people to make mistakes than to do better.

8. Fairness: I Don't Need to Negotiate for What I Want; I Just Want Fairness

Jana set herself up to be replaced. By demanding fair treatment, she was in effect asking Allen to change his own behavior or to fire her. Allen had no problem making that decision.

9. Excuses: There's a Good Reason

At least this is one Sacred Bull that Allen won't follow. When Dalton comes tomorrow, he won't have to hear any whining or excuses. Allen plans to go down with dignity. Dignity is all he has left. His Sacred Bulls caused him to do himself in.

10. Being Right: There's a Right Way and a Wrong Way; My Way Is Right

It never crossed Allen's mind that there may have been other ways to manage his department. He was convinced that his approach to management was the right way. Instead, Allen's way bred inefficiency and resentment. Jana and Richard also thought they were right. Look where that Bull got them.

ARE YOU FOLLOWING SACRED BULLS?

It's not only Allen who acts without thinking. We all do. We follow Sacred Bulls to protect ourselves:

We look out for Number One if we are convinced that no one else will act in our best interest.

We try to be perfect because we are afraid of the punishment for making mistakes.

We tell people what they want to hear because we think we can avert the unpleasantness of conflict.

The problem is that the things we do when we're following these Bulls often get us exactly what we are trying to avoid:

People who look out only for themselves make enemies.

Perfectionists make mistakes and cause other people to make even more.

Conflict-avoiders make more trouble for themselves.

Very few people would actually admit to following Sacred Bulls. The beliefs we *say* we live by are usually simpler and sound better than the ones we actually do live by. The only way to tell the difference is to look at our behavior and reason backwards. When we do that, we often see Sacred Bulls standing in the way.

How can you tell if you are following Sacred Bulls? *You know by how you feel.*

People who are following Sacred Bulls often feel worried, anxious, stuck, overwhelmed, even bored. Often they don't know the cause. They feel as if they have to deal with the same nagging problems over and over. Things never seem to go the way they should. There never seems to be anyone around who can really help them get things back on track.

We all have felt this way at times about our jobs and the people we work with. These occasional feelings of anger, irritation, anxiety, and boredom are completely normal. If, however, you have these feelings frequently, if they are becoming more intense or overwhelming, or if they are causing you problems at work, you're probably following one or more Sacred Bulls.

WHY YOU NEED THIS BOOK

Believing in Sacred Bulls can block you from reaching real effectiveness, satisfaction, and achievement. This book will show you how to start getting the things that everyone needs to be psychologically healthy and balanced:

- *A feeling of control over your own life*
- *A sense of accomplishment that comes from doing what is personally difficult*
- *A feeling of connection to and trust in other people*

Sacred Bulls do their worst damage in these three vital areas. They tell you that other people and other forces are calling the shots, that what you say and do has little influence over what happens to you. They convince you that what comes easy is all that's important, and that other people can't be trusted.

The best way to discover *your* Sacred Bulls is to look closely at what you do and what you feel, not at what you say. When you have learned to recognize and understand the Sacred Bulls in your life, you can take steps to change your behavior. This book will show you how.

A FIRST STEP

One of the first Sacred Bulls we must take by the horns is the notion that there is one right answer to every question. In some sections of this book, we do give you answers. We present straightforward lists of effective ways to handle the situations we describe. In other sections, as you will see, there are no lists. This is not because there are no right answers but because there are many. What's right depends on who you are and what you want to accomplish.

The problem in such situations is seldom that people can't decide what to do. In many cases they decide too easily without recognizing the choices available to them. Being too sure of what's right sometimes does more damage than not knowing.

That's the problem we address in the sections with no lists. Some readers may find this frustrating at first. But as they become more aware of the possibilities open to them, they are more likely to make the right choices for themselves.

It isn't easy but it's more effective. No Bull.

Chapter Two

THE BULL OF DENIAL
I Don't See the Problem,
So It Isn't There

*R*ob *doesn't understand why people just can't take a
joke. He thinks the office is altogether too serious, and
humor relieves tension, doesn't it? So he teases people occasionally.*

*His favorite audience is the women in the office. He says
things like, "A woman's place is in the kitchen, so could
you get me some coffee while you're there?" Or he might
tease another coworker with, "Did I hear snoring coming
out of your office when the door was closed?"*

He'll read pages from The Exceptionally Tasteless Joke
Book, *which is on permanent display on his desk, and he
loves to repeat crude comments that he heard his favorite
shock jock say on the radio the night before.*

*Rob thinks he's a real card. Everybody else thinks he's
an obnoxious, hostile jerk who uses his humor to attack
other people and then claims it was "just a joke." Rob
doesn't see it, so to him it's not there.*

Denial is the granddaddy of Sacred Bulls: "I don't see it, so it isn't there." This is the unconscious rule that makes all the others possible. We all edit our experience; we have to. There's too much going on every minute to pay attention to all of it. We see what we think is important and ignore everything else.

At its best, this editing can help us stay focused on what is important by ignoring irrelevant details. It becomes a problem when we edit out things that are painful or make us look bad instead of what is irrelevant. That is when we cross the line from editing into denying. At that point, we may not be able to see things that are very apparent and very important to other people. That's when what we don't see can hurt us.

Somebody ought to do something about a guy like Rob. You would. Rob's boss doesn't. People have complained to him hundreds of times, and he hasn't done a thing. The boss thinks that adults should work out their own interpersonal problems. He does not feel that management ought to intervene in every petty squabble that comes up. He has told Rob to tone it down. He wishes the whole department weren't so sensitive and would focus more on the job and less on little annoyances like Rob's indelicate sense of humor.

The official position is that the boss doesn't see a problem, so it isn't there.

In most companies, people are expected to use denial. Managers often see complaining as a worse problem than anything you might complain about. The official position is, "Everything is fine, and this is the best place in the world to work. If you don't agree, it's because you have a bad attitude."

Why Denial Is Such a Problem at Work

In most companies, people are expected to use denial. In business, being too reflective is often considered the same as being weak. If you think too much or admit too much, or if you express your emotions (other than a passion for excellence, of course), you may be considered unfit to lead. As a result, people rarely question basic assumptions. Things are what they are. Case closed, and get back to work.

Can you imagine arguing that you have no prejudices, no fears, and no bad habits, and that there is nothing that makes you unreasonably angry? Of course not. Yet that is probably what is expected of you on your job. At the very least, if you admitted to any of these human foibles, someone would accuse you of not doing your job correctly. So if you can't bring these human traits to work with you, where do they go? They go where everything else goes when you're not paying attention to it—on the back burner or in the low-priority pile. All too often they wind up sneaking up on you.

Although people are complex, their behavior is understandable and predictable. It should be the responsibility of managers to understand human behavior well enough so that efficiency is not compromised by needless conflict and resentment.

Managers should not have to make everybody happy, but they should see to it that people aren't so confused, frightened, or angry that their negative feelings impair their performance. We say this is a tremendous problem throughout the world of business. The Bull of Denial says, "What problem?"

Most of the people who own and run businesses are far more knowledgeable about economics and engineering than about human behavior. This is not a problem. (Psychologists and writers probably shouldn't be running corporations.) The problem comes when they assume there is nothing more they need to know about human behavior. If they don't see it, they assume it isn't there. (And you'd better assume the same thing if you want to keep climbing that career ladder.)

People who elsewhere in their lives make many of their decisions based on emotions and other irrationalities are expected to leave their doubts, feelings, and conflicting ideas at home. Their mission is to make decisions rationally for the good of the company, or at least consistent with the company line. (This is true even when the same company spends millions on advertising to influence the same irrational emotions in their customers.) In many businesses, denial is a part of doing your job.

At the firm, lawyers are expected to maintain a professional bearing at all times. You never take off your jacket, even in your own office. And you never air your doubts, even in the privacy of your own heart.

"Our main product is our clients' confidence in us. We cannot maintain that without confidence in ourselves." The founding partners said that eighty-five years ago, and it has been the gospel ever since. If you express doubt in the firm, in yourself, or in anything else, you're considered a loser. If you have any doubts, God forbid, you'd better keep them strictly to yourself.

The official position is: Nobody makes mistakes. If you make one, you're expected to cover it up on your own. If you see that someone else has made a mistake, you are expected to realize that this is not a matter for your concern. The rule of the day, every day, is black shoes, white shirts, and no dirty laundry.

At Victory, Inc., they never say die. They don't say "sick," either, or even "a little bit under the weather." You're expected to be awake, motivated, and at your desk every morning at eight o'clock. Oh, sure, Victory has sick leave, but you're expected to know enough not to use it for anything less than open-heart surgery.

If you want examples that are closer to home, look at the values statement or the policies and procedures manual for your own company. Chances are you'll see a lot of things that sound good but aren't the way people actually do things. (Discuss any discrepancies at your own peril.)

Denial Masquerades as Positive Thinking

Janice has high self-esteem. Every night before bedtime she repeats a list of self-affirmations: "I am a good person. I am a kind person. I care about other people. I am a good listener. I am a good manager." She learned this technique in a retreat workshop five years ago, and she'll be the first to tell you that it changed her life. She used to think she was not as good as the other managers in her group. Now her confidence has increased 110 percent.

The problem is, Janice is not as competent as the other managers in her group. She knows the theoretical stuff, but her personal style gets in her way. "Take care of your Inner Child and she'll take care of you." That is the rule Janice lives by, and that's what her employees are afraid of. Her Inner Child, not a grown-up manager, is running the department.

Her employees say Janice never listens, especially to things she doesn't want to hear. (Try telling her she made a mistake.) If you disagree with her, you're in for a good two hours of calm but persistent explanation of why you are wrong and Janice is right.

One of her favorite tricks (which she also learned at a retreat) begins whenever somebody says, "I assumed. . . ." Janice will write the word like this: ASS-U-ME. Then she will chirp, "If you assume, you make an ass out of you and me!"

She likes to give people "personal growth assignments." Recently she asked her staff to "go home and list all the problems you've had with authority figures in your past and state how they apply to the situation between you and me." (The fact that she is making some powerful assumptions is completely lost on her.)

Janice also plays favorites. If you're on her good side, you can do no wrong. But if the two of you aren't getting along, she will question your competence in all areas. Even worse, you can't get her to listen to what you have to say. When you don't feel what she expects you to feel, she will decide you are "in denial." Her employees may be in denial occasionally, but Janice lives there.

When Janice is not feeling threatened, she is a very nice person. Her employees aren't worried that she will fire them but that she will get her feelings hurt and make things difficult for everyone. When she perceives morale is low, she calls one of "those meetings" to discuss the situation and make all the criticisms go away.

At the end of the session you get the idea that she wants to have a group hug, but she's too sophisticated for that (thank God). Her official conclusion is, "All the complaints are out in the open and we are all working on our issues. So everything is resolved and back to normal." The fact is, for Janice and her employees, nothing has changed.

There is a line between positive thinking and denial. Janice is obviously way over that line. She uses whatever power she has in the situation to get rid of anything embarrassing or critical.

Her main agenda in her job is to be acknowledged as a good person and a good manager. Demanding the constant acknowledgment is precisely what prevents her from being a good manager. She forces people to say the things she wants to hear, then points to what they say as evidence that reality is as she would like it to be.

Janice uses her power to avoid seeing problems—they would only lower her self-esteem. It's the kind of trick only a Sacred Bull could love.

DENIAL CAN BE A REAL HEADACHE

Most people who work with Darien think he is inconsiderate, hostile, and downright rude. Darien thinks he has a problem with headaches. The pain in his head prevents him from seeing that he is another type of pain for everyone else.

Darien takes off his glasses and rubs the bridge of his nose. It's going to be a bad one; he knows already. These headaches just seem to come from nowhere, with no warning, and at the worst times. This meeting will last at least another half hour before Darien can get to his desk for his extra-strength tablets. Regular aspirin doesn't touch these babies. By then it will really be pounding.

Darien sneaks a glance at his watch. Then, after this damn meeting, he has about three days' worth of work due out this afternoon and about two hours left to get it done. What a day. A sigh escapes.

Austin, his boss, looks away from the charts he's presenting. "Is something wrong, Darien?"

"No, I'm fine, Austin. Just a little headache. I'll be okay."

A few people chuckle. Everybody in the room knows that Darien's headaches include a certain, shall we say, dramatic component. Darien is never one to suffer in silence. His headaches signal to everyone that he doesn't like what's going on.

True, the room is stuffy and Austin is not the most dynamic presenter, but he has some important points to make. There has been some foot tapping and coughing, and a few eyes have glazed over, but nobody can match Darien. His headaches deserve the Academy Award.

Austin starts presenting again, but attention is divided now between him and Darien. After all, Darien's show is better. He fidgets, massages his temples, rolls his eyes, snorts, and looks at his watch. He even starts stretching his neck muscles the way his doctor taught him.

Austin stops his presentation and fixes Darien with a cold stare. "As soon as you feel refreshed, Darien, I'll continue." His voice drips sarcasm, which Darien does not appreciate at all. He's dying for a pain tablet, and now Austin is picking on him. Darien simply cannot take it. With an injured smile, he says, "I'm terribly sorry, Austin," and leaves the meeting for the sanctuary of his office.

Austin, his stride hopelessly broken, wraps up his presentation with uncharacteristic haste, picks up his charts, and departs.

As soon as Austin leaves, the room is abuzz. "I can't believe Darien actually walked out!" "Did you see the look on Austin's face?"

Back in his office, Darien is beginning to calm down. Just taking the pain tablet seems to help his headache. Maybe he will get some work done this afternoon.

Darien is denying that he has an anger-control problem. Like many anger-related problems, his comes from a sense of time pressure. He can't stop thinking of all the work he has to finish. He gets angry if anything gets in the way of his doing it, and he lashes out by clearly showing his pain and impatience. The result is that he insults Austin, his boss. (Darien has a few problems with authority that he could stand to look at as well.)

If Austin were to confront him about his rude behavior, Darien would probably feel discriminated against. In his own mind, Darien is just a hardworking guy who gets headaches from the stress of his job. He doesn't see the anger, so it isn't there.

Unfortunately, anger is the part of Darien's personality that Austin and everyone else sees most clearly.

DENIAL IS A DEEP TRAP

Darien's case illustrates the deepest pitfall into which denial can lead. The more we avoid seeing something in ourselves, the more important it becomes. Whatever we are denying looms much larger than it would if we saw and dealt with it by other, more direct means. Darien is the kind of person who lashes out at anything that frustrates him, especially whatever seems like a waste of time when he is in a hurry. Darien is always in a hurry.

Darien does not see himself as an angry person. Angry people do damage, yell, threaten, pound the table, and call names when other people don't do what they want. Darien gets stressed out from all the demands placed on him, and that stress gives him headaches. To him, the headaches are more a badge of honor than a way of disguising hostility.

Darien's behavior is called passive-aggressive (which we will discuss in more detail in chapter 9). His headaches are real and painful. They are not all in his head (so to speak); they are psychosomatic. His arousal causes him to tighten the muscles in his jaw, neck, and forehead. (Try that for awhile, and you'll be convinced the pain is real.) Darien sees himself as a victim of the pain. He expects a little sympathy, but more often he gets retaliation, especially from the people whom he attacks, such as Austin.

Austin, by the way, is also following the Bull of Denial by ignoring the subtle cues that his audience is drifting. He does not have to think about this until somebody like

Darien does something blatant. Then, of course, Austin can hide behind the Bull and become a victim of rudeness. It is always easier to see the things that other people do to us rather than the things we do to other people. Therefore, Austin does not have to reexamine his image of himself as a dynamic speaker.

In groups, other people's unconscious behaviors regulate each other, and no one has to talk or even think about them. We learn to do this in our families. Few of us think a lot about why we do what we do. Instead, we often feel ourselves reacting in physical or emotional ways that often make the situation worse. We believe we are just doing what any reasonable person would do. We seldom ask ourselves why.

THIS BULL HAS THREE PARTS

Few of us regularly think about our own motivations. If we don't see them, we believe they aren't there. Instead, we learn to sidestep the hulking Bull that everyone else can see. Darien's story illustrates the four elements of denial common to people who honor this Sacred Bull, no matter how badly he tramples their lives.

1. They see themselves as they would like to be rather than as they are. *What you allow yourself to experience depends on how you define yourself, especially on how you think you* should *be.*

If new information is inconsistent with this definition, you may work very hard to protect yourself from this knowledge. For example, Darien defines himself as so dedicated that the stress of his job gives him headaches. He cannot see the headaches as his method of fighting back against people who are in his way, waste his time, or pick on him. If they take offense, he has more evidence that he is being unfairly attacked.

2. They believe other people cause their feelings. *Emotions come from inside yourself, not from external situations or from "out of nowhere."*

Other people cannot make you angry (or give you headaches). The slow economy cannot make you depressed. Your own thoughts have to intervene. Darien is always thinking about how much he has to do and how little time he has to do it in. This leads to a general feeling of resentment. If you pinned him down, he might say people who waste his time give him a pain. Actually his resentment is what makes his head hurt. He builds up pressure inside by saying things like "I can't believe I have to sit through this meeting when I have so much work to do."

This is why Sacred Bulls have so much power. They determine how we define a situation and what we see as important. That, in turn, will determine how we feel and what we do.

3. They assume that what they see is all there is. *The beliefs you live by will determine what you see and what you don't see, what you define as important and unimportant.*

You see what you expect to see. Of course, what you see confirms your expectations. In the situations that are most difficult for you, this creates a closed loop. You cannot see around the Bull of Denial to what else may be out there. No wonder you end up feeling stuck. Often there is a way out, but it lies in looking at things you haven't been allowing yourself to see.

In the rest of this book, we will demonstrate how Sacred Bulls make you think and act in ways that lead to negative behavior and feelings of frustration, ineffectiveness, and depression. (Even if you don't call them by these names, you'll still get all the destructive perks that come with these emotions. Darien, for example, does not define his feelings as anger, but he gets the discomfort, tension, and alienation that anger creates.)

Using Denial to Do Unto Others

Mike is always saying, "If you don't understand the politics around here, it can kill you." You usually hear this spiel when he's in your office, behind closed doors. He's explaining how a certain person is trying to gain enough support to make his play for a bigger share of the departmental pie, or to grab control of the votes on the projects committee, or some other Machiavellian move that will destroy the balance of departmental power. If you waver or hesitate instead of agreeing with him, Mike usually has just the right extra bit of dirt on the other person to win you over.

To Mike, it's always a defensive game. People are always out to get something that doesn't belong to them. Even now they're getting their allies together to make their move!

You have to take a step back to see that Mike is doing exactly what he is accusing other people of doing: lining up support and trying to keep somebody from gaining too much power. If you're speaking of politicians who can kill you, put Mike's name at the top of the list.

Yet Mike is the guy who is always taking a position against the sneaky double-dealing that's going on around here. Is he putting on an act?

Mike is probably doing less acting than you think. One of the best ways to keep yourself from seeing what's going on in your own head is to believe that it's going on in someone else's. The technique is called *projection*, and it gives you an excuse to do unto others before they do unto you. (Most of the great acts of aggression in history were done in the name of defense.)

Mike sees himself as a nice guy, the last bastion of defense against the ruthless politicians. What he doesn't see is that all of his actions tend to serve his own interest and to be just as ruthless and underhanded as the actions he expects from the politicians. (This is like trying to fight a fire by throwing gasoline on it.) It is always easier to see what others are doing to you than to look at what you are doing.

DEALING WITH OTHER PEOPLE'S SACRED BULL

How do you deal with people like Darien, Janice, and Mike who are deluding themselves about their own actions and motivations? If you want to have any kind of positive effect on them, you first have to stop thinking of them as hypocrites or referring to them as hypocrites. (If, however, you simply want to talk about them behind their backs or make them really angry in person, the word *hypocrite* was invented for just this purpose.)

Don't waste your time trying to convince Darien that he is angry, or that Janice is abusing power, or that Mike is a Machiavelli wannabe. They won't get it. *You* may see it, but they don't.

To be effective, you will have to learn to operate within their own definition of themselves and to enlarge that definition to include the kinds of thoughts you want them to consider.

"I See You Are Concerned About This"

People like Darien see themselves not as angry people but as busy people, dedicated people, even put-upon people. If you want to know what's bothering them, give their anger another, more neutral name. *Upset* and *concerned* are words that people like Darien usually will accept. You might begin the conversation by saying, "I see you are concerned about this." (Do *not* say, "I see you are *angry* about this." If you lead off with this, you will run smack into the Sacred Bull.)

Darien's discontent seems to result from his feeling of time pressure. You will need to show him how attending a meeting (or whatever the actual situation) will save him time in the long run. Often people like Darien gain inordinate power because their minds are so easy to read. When Darien starts looking at his watch during a meeting, the speaker's natural response is to speed up. Darien gets what he wants without asking. You will be more in control of the situation if you can get him to ask for what he wants rather than just acting on it for him. (Many people who behave like Darien are also perfectionists, which we will discuss in detail in chapter 8.)

"You're Right"

People like Janice, the manager who uses positive thinking to block out all her faults, see themselves as kind, caring colleagues. They believe they listen well and just happen to be *right* all the time (a characteristic we will discuss in detail in chapter 11). If they weren't, they feel they wouldn't fit in. What they want is friendship and belonging.

Getting angry at them will not help. They want you to pay attention to them, compliment, listen to, and ask them for help and advice. They also lap up bald-faced flattery. This is what they think acceptance means.

Consider dealing with them by focusing on the positive whenever possible: give them as much of what they want as is reasonable. They will repay your flattery with loyalty, support, and probably more self-improvement tapes than you want to hear. People like Janice are so bound by their definition of themselves as "wonderful" that they can be easily influenced through compliments.

"Go Talk to Him"

People like Machiavellian Mike take an active hand in creating the reality they say they fear and hate. Encourage them to look at their goals and show how they can come closer to reaching them through cooperating. *Your* goal is to try to convince them that allying with their "enemy du jour" will actually help them get what they want.

Mike's Sacred Bull keeps him away from the people he is afraid to confront. Instead, he attacks them safely in your office, with the door closed. The more you encourage him to get out and deal with them, the more effective he will be and the less often he will come trying to enlist your help in his conspiracies. You can say persuasively, "Go talk to him, Mike. You know: Get close to him. Find out what he's thinking so you can be more effective in stopping his plot."

DENIAL IS NOT GOOD FOR YOUR PSYCHOLOGICAL HEALTH

Denial makes you look at only one side of an issue and ignore the others. This can block you from getting what you need to stay psychologically healthy and balanced. In chapter 1, we identified three elements necessary to maintain psychological health:

- The feeling that you are in control of what happens to you
- A sense of challenge and growth, which comes from trying to do things that are difficult for you
- A feeling of connection to other people

The Sacred Bull of Denial makes it easy to misinterpret events and thereby miss opportunities to grow in these areas. The human tendency to believe "I don't see a problem, so it isn't there" is most likely to surface when things go wrong. It is particularly easy to blame change itself, rather than your own lack of adapting to change, as the cause of the problem.

"Don't Blame Me"

Most of us want to think of ourselves as good people: competent, talented, and hardworking. If we are willing to take responsibility for what happens to us, we also end up having to live with the self-blame if things go wrong. In the short term it may seem easier to use denial to convince ourselves that it wasn't our fault. The price, however, is losing the perception that we have some control over what happens.

The market is soft. That's why Jerry's sales totals are down. (So are everybody else's.) He's working harder than ever, but people are just hanging on tighter to their money. The experts may say the recession is over, but in Jerry's market everybody is still being very cautious.

If Jerry looks at the situation in this way, he may not recognize what control he does have. He will be less likely to explore new sales techniques and approaches to deal with softer market conditions. Instead, he can hide behind the Bull of Denial, a victim of the economy.

Art has talent and ability. He could go far in the business if it weren't for the bosses he's been stuck with. Over the past five years he's had three, and—if you can believe it— each was worse than the last. None of them recognized Art's potential (as if they could recognize anything).

If you want to hear all about it and have a few hours to spare, Art has hundreds of entertaining anecdotes. He doesn't have the success he deserves, but at least he has some good stories about why that isn't his fault.

Art is missing the fact that one of the most important aspects of success in any field is learning how to develop a good working relationship with your boss. If you can't do that, all the talent in the world won't get you very far.

Of course, everyone is controlled to some extent by outside forces. Denying that can be damaging, too. You have to recognize the outside factors. Once you do, however, it's time to figure out what you can do within those limits to accomplish your goals. If you can't do this, you'll be stuck believing that if you were meant to fly, you would have been born with wings.

Moving Toward Challenge—or Away?

Challenge involves doing what is difficult instead of what comes easily. Challenge is essential to psychological health. If you aren't challenged, you can feel depressed. Your job seems less interesting, you become less motivated, you feel less capable, and you become less willing to take any risks to change your situation.

We all want a little peace and quiet, but as a steady diet it doesn't provide most of us with enough to live on. (This is why some people experience psychological or physical problems soon after they retire.) Without challenge, life goes gray and dull. Nevertheless, most of us regularly avoid challenge because it's difficult, risky, and intimidating. We see the pain, and that's enough to blind us to the possible gain. For many people in business, this Sacred Bull of Denial can help people turn questions of *change* into issues of good versus evil.

Managed competition indeed! Joan thinks the very words sound like some insidious disease. She didn't go to medical school to have some bean counter dictate how she should run her practice. Risk sharing. Utilization review. Capitation. All the jargon boils down to is doing as little as

*possible and making more money for insurance compa-
nies. Well, Joan is having none of it.*

*All her colleagues are joining together into group prac-
tices and kowtowing to third-party payees. Not Joan. She's
going to do things the way she always has, in her own
practice. If she gets dropped from the insurance company
panels, so be it. There will always be people who will want
to pay the price to see a* real *doctor.*

Joan sounds like a saint, doesn't she? Exactly the kind
of doctor you'd want taking care of you. Someone who
resists the pressure to conform. Someone who stands up
to the bureaucrats. But is Joan really taking the hard
road, or is her tough rhetoric actually covering resistance
to change?

As a health-care provider, does Joan know all she needs
to know about efficiency? Can closer review of her cases
reveal nothing positive? She makes staying out of a group
practice sound like a virtue, especially to herself. Several
years from now, however, when her number of patients
has dramatically decreased, will she still feel as good
about the choice she is making now? By resisting managed care, is Joan taking the hard road or the easy one?

It is not always easy to tell whether you're running
toward challenges or away from them. (You will find
further discussion of this topic in the next chapter, on
Blind Spots and Shortcuts.)

Loyalty? Isn't That for Chumps?

Nowhere is independence more highly prized than in
business. To succeed in most business cultures, you have
to demonstrate your ability to recognize and act on important information that no one ever tells you. The thinking goes, if you're sharp, you'll figure out what you're
supposed to do without support from above. (The people

who manage you presumably have more important things to do than explain your job to you.)

One of the things you'd better figure out is how to take care of yourself. Your boss may be feeling strong pressure to pay attention to the economic aspects of managing rather than the messier and more subtle human dynamics. The Bull of Denial will say, "Take care of the money. The people will take care of themselves."

If managers continue to manage the money and expect people to manage themselves, they dispense with such old-fashioned issues as loyalty and trust. The Sacred Bull of Denial helps managers dismiss these qualities as mere signs of overdependency. As you will see in chapter 4, it also offers free rein to another Sacred Bull: "Look out for Number One."

Jeff, a middle manager, is what people thirty years ago might have called a "company man." He's been working at Victory, Inc., for sixteen years and believes, "If you take care of your company, it will take care of you." He accepts all assignments without complaint, even the grunt work that holds no flashiness or challenge, and does the best job he can.

During hard times, Jeff accepted no raises. A few years ago, when the company hit a very rough patch, he even took a salary cut. He didn't try to display himself as a martyr either. He recognizes that the company's needs have to come first, even if he and his coworkers have to take a few setbacks.

One morning Jeff arrived at his office and found a memo on his desk: The functions of his entire department were being contracted out to an overseas firm. A pink slip arrived soon after the memo.

Of course Jeff feels betrayed and angry about losing his job. But something more subtle is also going on in his mind. After the anger subsides, as he tries to make sense of what went wrong, Jeff will come to the inevitable conclusion that he was stupid to be so trusting. Loyalty is for chumps, he decides. The smart people look out for themselves.

The management of Jeff's company looked first and only at the economics of the situation. They didn't see any economic value in loyalty from people like Jeff (so, of course, it isn't there).

This scenario is being played out thousands of times a day: companies seeing no value in loyalty, and all of us coming to realize that if we have any feelings of loyalty we had better deny them or we'll be played for suckers. Something important is slipping away, even if we don't choose to look at it. That "something" is the feeling of connection and trust. The Bull of Denial says it just isn't economically feasible in this market.

IS THERE A BULL YOU CAN'T SEE?

How do you know whether people think *you* are refusing to see the Sacred Bull of Denial? You could try asking them, but if you are deep into denial you might not hear the answer. Instead, a good place to start is with one of Grandfather's favorite sayings: "If three people call you a horse, buy a saddle." If you have gotten the same feedback from three different people and you still don't believe it, this book is for you.

The Denial List

An effective strategy is to try on the uncomfortable information for awhile to see if it fits. Ask yourself, "If what this persons says were true, how would I know? What would I see? How would I act?" To help you find your Sacred Bull, consider the following list of difficult questions that represent the things that people most often deny:

- *What things make you unreasonably angry?*
- *What are your bad habits?*
- *What things are you afraid of doing or saying?*
- *What were your biggest mistakes?*
- *Against what ideas and people are you prejudiced?*

Go ahead. Make your list. Actually write down your answers. We'll wait.

If you end up with fewer than five responses for each question, the chances are good that some denial is in operation. This is how denial feels when it happens: You don't feel anything. It's not that you purposely closed your eyes. You just forgot to include some things, or you really couldn't come up with any more. For at least one of the questions, you probably couldn't think of *any* answer, and you probably still can't.

Maybe you distanced yourself from the task by misunderstanding the questions to be less personal. We all get angry, for example, at "people who don't do their jobs," and everybody is afraid that "interest rates will go up."

Because you couldn't figure out five answers to each question, does that mean there really is nothing appropriate that fits? We bet your boss, your employees, your coworkers would easily be able to fill in the list that you may have forgotten!

Part of being human is having attributes that you can't see or, at least, that you experience differently. Other people certainly may experience you in a way that is inconsistent with your own definition of yourself. If you believe that this automatically means that they are wrong and you are right, and that there is nothing you can learn from their perceptions, we can guarantee that the Sacred Bull of Denial has free rein in your life (or free reign— we guarantee the Bull will take charge).

Even if you are self-blaming in some areas, and one or two of your lists are very long, this doesn't mean that you are free from denial. Ask yourself what you are doing about the things on your list. There is a time-honored strategy of dealing with problems by admitting to everything and doing nothing. The things you admit but don't consider important enough to act on may cause as much trouble as the things you don't think about at all.

Five Ways to Detect Denial

Denial can happen to you; but when it does, you won't know for sure unless you pay attention. (How's that for contradiction?) There are, however, a few cues you can watch for in your own behavior that usually indicate there's more to what's going on than you think. The following signs indicate you may be artificially simplifying the world to fit the way you think you ought to be:

1. *You find yourself arguing vigorously about someone else's perception of you.* In this situation, there is much more to learn than whether you are right and the other person is wrong. The key is to keep your defensiveness under control.

Even if you are not yelling or pounding the table, you may not be listening. You may be too busy thinking strongly that the other person is dead wrong. If you disagree, you need to listen. Think about what the other person is describing. You may be surprised at the new view you gain of your own behavior.

This advice also holds true for opinions about issues so close to you that you consider them a part of yourself. Many people, for example, carry adamant ideas about what their job is supposed to be, ideas that are very different from those of people at different levels—their boss or their subordinates. This can lead to all sorts of conflicts and "personality issues" that could be avoided if they considered what the picture looks like from other people's point of view.

2. *You have an annoying habit or an addiction.* For every one person who comments on it, there are probably ten people who agree but are afraid to say anything. If you wonder if something you do is a problem, and then decide it isn't, you're probably the only person being fooled. If it's important enough for you to think about it, it's serious enough to do something about it, too.

3. *You frequently joke about the same person or group at work.* For most of us, the things we joke about are the things we have the most to learn about. Do you think people who play office politics are funny? Do you joke about other departments and their pettiness, or laugh about how some people just don't understand how the system operates? This is an excellent indication that you need to learn more about how these people view the world.

The same is even more true for the people or ideas you hold in contempt. If you feel angry because you work with people who are weak, angry, or stupid, this may indicate that you have a more serious problem than the joking indicates. (See chapter 6 for a discussion of blame.) You don't have to agree with other people's positions. You do need to understand them and recognize their importance to the people who hold these views.

4. *You find yourself saying, "That's a great idea, but we can't afford it right now."* If it's really a great idea, you can't afford *not* to do it.

5. *You typically pass off some points of view as ill-informed or biased.* "That's what all the liberals say." "Republicans never understand." "Employees don't see the big picture." "That's what management wants you to believe." People who hold these beliefs, so different from your own, have the most to teach you. Seek them out and learn from them. Even if it makes your life more complicated at first, it may also make you more effective. Certainly it will help protect you from the Sacred Bull of Denial: "I don't see it, so it isn't there."

Chapter Three

THE BULL OF BLIND SPOTS
AND SHORTCUTS
What I Don't Like
Can't Be Important

C asey could have been a contender—not in the ring, but in the corporate arena. When he got his first job after receiving his MBA, Casey seemed destined to go straight to the top. His skill at sales is the stuff legends are made of. He loves talking to people. He's direct and open. People trust him instinctively—and they buy from him. Casey set records that are still unbroken in every department he worked in.

He was the youngest person ever promoted to district sales manager—eight years ago. Since then he has been passed over for every promotion.

Casey's subordinates don't understand why he isn't CEO by now. To them he's one of the all-time great salesmen. He likes nothing better than going out with a sales rep, actually working with customers, showing how it's done. His favorite trick is to take a rep into a territory that the rep thinks is completely covered then come up with new business out of thin air.

That is what Casey thinks his job is all about. And that is his problem. Headquarters disagrees.

What is the most important part of your job? If you're like most people, you have strong feelings on this subject. Probably the part you consider most important is the part you're best at.

We hope you're right. You wouldn't want to make a mistake on such a crucial issue. So we think we should warn you: There's a Sacred Bull out there who convinces people that the parts of their work that they don't like doing, aren't good at, or are afraid of are not really what the job is about.

This is the Patron Bull of Blind Spots and Shortcuts, the one that says, "What I don't like can't be important." This Bull seems to make perfectly good sense because, like all Sacred Bulls, he tells you exactly what you want to believe. If you listen to him, you might end up doing some real damage to your career.

Casey Strikes Out

To the people at headquarters, Casey's job involves a lot of time in front of the computer doing forecasts, regressions, and market share analyses, then presenting them with elaborate graphics at divisional meetings. Casey has always thought this practice was kind of funny. "I feel like I wandered into a convention of mathematicians," he jokes.

At divisional meetings he argues passionately that managers can become too obsessed with numbers. "The numbers only reflect what's going on out there in the territories," he says. "You can't make the numbers grow by sitting at a computer. You have to get out there, meet the customers, and find out what they need. You have to work with sales reps and teach them that the real action is bringing in new business. That's how the numbers will grow!"

Upper management is not impressed. They think the days of a smile and a shoeshine are long gone. They believe in centralized marketing, identifying demographic niches, and going after specific targets. You don't just go out knocking on doors to drum up new business any more. Sales managers are supposed to be working with data. *The people who are promoted are the ones who can forecast trends and look at data in new ways.*

The truth is, Casey is scared to death of computers. He was never particularly good at math, so he developed himself in other areas. He laughs at all the "fancy stuff" the company does with numbers. He says pretty soon they'll learn it's the basics—the face-to-face contact—that makes or breaks a company. That's the part Casey is great at. It's the part he likes, the part that comes easy for him. He ignores and downplays the parts he doesn't like and doesn't understand.

It irks him that the company has passed him over so many times. His district has good numbers and a motivated team. It's a first-rate training ground. Every other district is clamoring for Casey-trained reps.

The company sees value in what Casey does, but it is not the kind of work they consider appropriate for an upper-level manager. To the Sales Division at headquarters, Casey is making a choice to avoid the number-crunching and analytic responsibilities of a serious manager in favor of his role as Super Sales Rep. That's okay with them. He's doing fine—right where he is.

Casey keeps applying for promotions and has been told many times what he needs to do. At headquarters he has the reputation of being a tough sell for new ideas. Casey sees it as being true to his own values and, he might add, to the values that made this company great. It is a point of pride with him. He wants acceptance for what he is and what he means to the company. He's a sales rep, not a mathematician!

He looks at the latest set of graphs and analyses from the Sales Division at headquarters and shakes his head. He just can't see why this stuff is so big-time important.

Like most people, Casey has some real blind spots about the things he's not good at. He just can't see what's so important about them. His situation would have been very different if he had said to himself, "I don't like numbers and I'm scared of computers. So I'll just stay away from them and pay the price—a dead-end, lower-level management job." At least he would feel he had made a choice. He could have learned to live with it and be satisfied.

It is natural to find yourself avoiding the things you find most difficult. The danger is in what you tell yourself about the things you avoid. If you're following the Bull of Shortcuts, you probably have convinced yourself that you've done a great job of arranging your life. The things you find difficult are not terribly essential for success. What you don't like can't really be important.

THE BULL'S BLINDING POWER

This is where the blind spots come in. We all want to think of ourselves as good people doing a good job. It is difficult for most of us to admit, "I know this is critical, but I don't like it so I'm not going to do it. I'll just accept the consequences." With the help of a little Bull, most of us quietly slip the things that give us the most difficulty into a lower priority slot and go on to the things we consider more important. Presto! The problem is gone!

"I don't see it, so it can't be there." The blinding power of these Bulls is amazing.

Renee doesn't seem to know which direction is up. In her company, which is heavily marketing and sales driven, virtually all the top managers have spent some time in sales or marketing. Renee had a couple of chances to move to sales but declined. She doesn't like sales and never has. It feels demeaning, like being paid to be phony.

She'd never admit it, of course, but Renee thinks sales is a little scary. There's so much pressure: meeting quotas, making cold calls, getting rejected by strangers every day. She didn't get her hard-won degree just for the pleasure of having people hang up on her over and over. Renee has dynamite interpersonal skills and extensive training, but how can she connect with people whose faces she can't even see? They're just voices on the phone, not even listening.

Her ambition is to be manager of the Human Resources Department. She knows she could really make a difference in a job so perfect for her talents. She has been waiting for an opening to come up there, but there have been no openings. She doesn't realize that there are never *openings in HR. The director and her assistant have been there for years, and the rest of the department keeps getting downsized.*

The other problem, although Renee doesn't know it, is that if a management position did open up in HR, she wouldn't get it because she hasn't spent the requisite time in sales or marketing.

Renee's career is stalled because she expected she could get to the top just as she was, without making any personal changes. She did not develop herself by confronting her fear of sales. When Human Resources, her first choice for promotion, did not work out, Renee did not choose a different path that would have forced her to learn to do things she didn't want to do.

She could have learned from these kinds of moves, but instead Renee structured her career so that she has never really had to grow professionally. She did not even try to transfer to another company where her style might have been more rewarded because she didn't want to take the risk.

Renee has not learned the first principle of upward mobility: *No matter who you are or where you are, the way up involves doing things you don't like, are afraid of, or think are irrelevant.* Aside from winning the lottery, no other way exists.

THE FEAR OF SELLING

Renee suffers from a common fear: the fear of selling. Selling is *hard*. You have to be outgoing and persistent, you have to make a good impression, you have to ask people for things, and you have to be able to be told no and not be devastated. These are difficult skills to master unless, like Casey, you're born with them. For most of us even comedy is easy compared with selling. No wonder so many of us say to ourselves, "I'm a [your occupation]. I shouldn't have to sell." This is an example of USDA prime Bull. In any job there are many tasks you won't really want to do but you will have to do them to succeed. One of these is selling.

The personnel officer smiles and says, "Tell me about yourself." Connie is on. She has rehearsed her response, and she's ready to convince Personnel (and the vice president who will interview her next) that she is the only person for the job. They'd be crazy not to hire her!

It's not a sales job, but Connie will have to "sell" herself to get it.

Gary from Engineering has a new idea that might save a bundle in the manufacturing process. He has a few sketches and some rough projections to show Paul, the production manager. Gary knows he needs Paul in his corner if this idea has a chance to go anywhere.

Gary has to sell his idea to Paul, or nobody will buy it.

Marlene, an attorney, is meeting with a group of clients who could hand her a very big case. Will she get it? It depends on what they think of her. Besides the air of professional competence that Marlene usually projects, she also makes a special effort to show that she can listen and be concerned with what her clients want. She wants them to decide that they need her on this case because she cares.

It's subtle—Marlene wouldn't have it any other way—but it's still selling.

Aaron knows particle physics, that's for sure. People don't become assistant professors without knowing their stuff. But it takes more than that to get tenure. So Aaron is polishing the grant proposal he'll be mailing in the morning. Without grants, there will be no research; without research, no publication; without publication, no tenure. That's even simpler than particle physics.

Aaron needs to sell the funding sources on his ideas or he won't be doing any particle physics.

None of the people in these examples is a sales rep. Nevertheless, to be successful, each of them needs to use the same skill: selling. It is never enough merely to have what it takes. You always have to convince other people. The world of business is based on selling. It is the one skill that everyone needs. If you think your job does not require selling, we know what Bull you've been listening to!

Skipping the "People Skills"

"People skills"—empathy, sensitivity, and the ability to deal with feelings—come easily to some. To others they are difficult, draining, and even a little frightening. To them the Bull of Shortcuts whispers, "Don't worry. We're at *work* here. Feelings are completely irrelevant."

Jillian sees herself as a "Dragnet" type: Just the facts, ma'am. She has no patience with employees who let their feelings get in the way of the work they have to do. To her, emotional means weak, soft, sentimental, easily exploited, and totally unable to do the job. She'll have none of it from her subordinates or from herself. It's unprofessional. Jillian believes in telling people what to do, then expecting them to do it. She doesn't care how they feel about it.

Jillian sees her demeanor as unsentimental and business-like. She thinks a manager has to make hard decisions, and feelings would just get in the way. She criticizes her peers for paying too much attention to employee complaints or being concerned about what their subordinates might think about every issue. She sees this as conduct unbecoming a manager. She has work to do and goals to attain, and she's not going to let sniveling get in the way.

Jillian doesn't make small talk, period. She doesn't have time for it. Let other managers waste time talking about the weather, sports, and whose daughter had a baby. Jillian would rather do something productive with her time. Never mind that she is seen as so aloof that most people in the company would rather not work with her. Who needs them? If they can't cut it, maybe they should transfer to another department.

Jillian believes that her lack of sentimentality is a virtue. It helps her as a manager, especially when she has to make difficult choices between money and people.

Actually, her sentiments cost money, particularly in turnover. Jillian's turnover rate is the highest in the company.

Many people not only believe that the things they don't like are unimportant but also manage to convince themselves that they are virtuous for avoiding them. Such is the power of the Sacred Bull. It can turn reality on its head and make you believe the opposite of what is true. One of the main functions of these creatures is to protect you from having to change.

Jillian does have emotions, but they are buried beneath a layer of frost as thick as a polar ice cap. She thinks if she allows one tiny crack in the ice, all her feelings will come flooding out. She doesn't have to worry. A hockey team could skate on her professional facade.

Underneath the ice is a fear of failure so frightening to Jillian that she will destroy her effectiveness to protect herself from it. All the while she believes that her aloofness is merely professional distance.

THE WORKAHOLIC HABIT

Work is so important in most of our lives that we can use it to distract ourselves from all kinds of other problems and difficulties. Perhaps that's why there are so many workaholics. For them, work is easier than most of the other things they might do with their time.

Clay is the first to admit that he's a workaholic (but his admission sounds more like boasting than confessing a fault). He likes to say that his work is his hobby, which is lucky, because he has no other interests. For Clay, existence has three parts: working, having nothing to do, and sleeping. When he comes home from work, he mows the lawn.

On weekends, he works on house repairs. (There's always some job that needs doing if you look for it, he always says.)

Of course, nobody appreciates all the work he does, particularly his boss. He pays more attention to the office politicians than to Clay, a guy who still knows how to do a day's work. What Clay can't understand is how the slackers can get away with all their goofing off. The boss always seems ready to listen to their stupid jokes. They're the ones the boss asks to join him for his fancy lunches downtown, while Clay gets a vague nod on the boss's way out the door. Well, that's okay. Nobody ever handed Clay anything. No reason to think things should start changing now. At least he knows, inside himself, that he's doing the job the way it should be done.

Clay is right that he gets no appreciation. The fact is, he's a bore. He doesn't have the ghost of a sense of humor, and his idea of a conversation is pointing out to people how they could be doing something better. The saddest part, as his boss recognizes, is that Clay is not a first-rate worker, either. To Clay, doing a job in the shortest amount of time smacks of laziness. It's *work* that he values, so why should he do anything to make less of it? If he keeps busy enough, he won't have to look at all the things he's ignoring—such as his lack of social skills.

Laurie's office walls are covered with plaques and commendations. Everybody in her company admits they couldn't get along without her. Her coworkers love her, and her bosses promote her. At work she's charming, considerate, and efficient. She seems to float through her day, graceful as a swan gliding across the water.

But when she unlocks her apartment door at the end of the day, Laurie feels like a swan on land—clumsy, out of balance and, worst of all, not in control. Her nights at

*home are just hours to endure until her real life begins
again the next morning in the office.*

At work there are people who praise her. That is where
Laurie shines. She knows what she's doing at work. The
world outside the office is too complicated, too unpredictable, too much outside her control. If her boss would
let her, Laurie would work every Saturday, too. Then she
wouldn't have to worry about all those long, shapeless
hours to fill.

*Steve doesn't really like work. The last thing he'd call
himself is a workaholic. He'd love to take some time off,
but there are just too many things that need to be done.
(And he needs the money. Ask him how much it costs to
raise a family these days.)*

*Take a vacation? Sure, just as soon as he wins the lottery.
For now, there's too much to do. He's still catching up
from last month, when his wife forced him to stay home
for three days with the flu.*

*Steve will take a well-deserved break just as soon as he
reasonably can. But this is the busiest time of the year. It's
just crazy how, every time he finishes one task, two new
ones seem to jump onto his desk.*

Workaholics have a difficult time recovering from this
addiction, especially when they're always getting rewarded for it with a secret sense of superiority, or plaques
on the wall, or the certainty that they are indispensable.
True workaholics can convince themselves that the other
things in life, which don't come as easily to them (such as
developing relationships, perhaps) are not as important.
Workaholics are actually doing what comes easily to
them—working—and ignoring the things in their lives
that are harder.

SACRED BULL DICTATES MANAGEMENT STYLE

Management is at best an ambiguous task. Ask any ten managers to define *management* and you'll get ten different answers. Sometimes the Bull of Shortcuts convinces them that management consists of doing what comes naturally to them and ignoring the other parts of the job that are "just not important." There are three different areas you can manage: money, people, and task. Most managers have a preference for one and sometimes blind spots for the others.

Craig believes the divinely ordained task of management is cost control. His budget is his bible. He can quote it line and verse. Accounting is his forte, and paying close attention to line items is his secret of success. His eyes are fixed on this quarter's bottom line. He's always on the lookout for how to save a little here or there. If he takes care of the money, the rest will take care of itself.

Craig is a very frustrating person to work for. Any time you suggest anything, his only question is, "How much does it cost?" It rarely crosses his mind to consider, "Will it do the job better?" or "Will people like it?" He assumes it is somebody else's job to worry about the answers to those questions.

Dennis cares about how the people in his department feel about their jobs. His theory of management is simple: Satisfied workers do high-quality work. He sees his job as keeping his employees satisfied. He makes sure they have sufficient direction, equipment that doesn't break down, a chance to participate in decisions and, most of all, a manager who's willing to listen.

He majored in psychology and really enjoys helping people with their problems. When there are interpersonal disputes in his department, he's in his element. He takes them seriously and works them through, no matter how much time it takes. That's probably why his productivity figures are some of the lowest in the division.

Dennis knows his numbers are down and he's working on it, but you can't measure the value of cohesion in money. It takes time to develop a team that really knows how to work together. Dennis has been at it six years, and he's just getting started.

Wendy is an engineer by training and by proclivity. She's great at knowing what needs to happen, in what order, and by whom to get the job done. She is possibly the most organized human being in the Western Hemisphere—which is what managing is to her: keeping everything organized, on time, and done right.

"Right" is, of course, defined as Wendy's way. New ideas can sometimes confuse the process. She doesn't have many, and she expects the same courtesy from you.

If you work for Wendy, you'll get along fine if you listen carefully and do what you're told. To her the task is what's important, not what it costs or how you feel about it.

All of these managers are doing their jobs right. And wrong.

Every manager has to manage all three: the money, the people, and the job. This is what makes managing such an elusive and difficult skill. Every time you try to narrow it down, you miss something important. The problem is that most managers tend to focus on the parts that bring out their own natural skills and talents and to ignore the parts that they find difficult. They also tend to see the way that is easiest for them as the "right" way and to have little patience with people who use a different approach.

None of the three styles sketched above is complete. Each runs into predictable problems. Shortcuts always lead to blind spots.

- Money managers, like Craig, usually are great with this quarter's bottom line, but they tend to have long-term problems with morale, turnover, and quality control. Of course, these problems affect dollars in the long run.
- People managers, like Dennis, often have staffs with high morale and creativity, but they sometimes run into problems with the bottom line.
- Task managers, like Wendy, may have stable and efficient operations that do very well with defined tasks, but such managers are often limited to their own understanding of the situation. They often have a hard time with the idea that there is more than one way to market a product. They aren't particularly skillful at letting their people solve problems. Of the three types, the task managers are the least able to deal effectively with change. When the job is complex and change-able, these managers are the ones who crash first.

The Sacred Bull of Shortcuts and Blind Spots will try to convince you that there is one best way to manage—the way that is easiest for you. It is always tempting to believe that what is most difficult for you is unimportant. Giving in to that temptation can cause you major problems.

To manage effectively, you must be able to manage money, people, and task. Most managers are better at one of those areas than the others. That is not the problem. It only becomes a problem if, instead of telling yourself you need to work especially hard on the areas you're weakest in, you begin to believe those areas don't matter.

The best managers regularly consult colleagues with different approaches when they run into problems. They try to anticipate and discuss potential problems before they occur. They recognize that diverse approaches are the only protection they have from their own blind spots.

THE BULL'S SECRET WEAPON

What makes this Bull so powerful? How can he convince people that it's all right to ignore important details of their jobs, even when it's clear to everyone else that they aren't taking care of business?

The answer is fear. People will accept almost any rationalization that will allow them to avoid something they're afraid of. The best rationalizations—the kind this Bull is famous for—are the ones that prevent you from realizing that you're afraid of anything. If something is irrelevant, you never have to get close enough to it to realize you're afraid of it. It's a neat trick, and it explains why this Bull has so much power in so many businesses.

What most business people fear most is feeling incompetent. We all work hard to maintain an internal picture of ourselves as competent people who are able to do what we should do and know what we should know. When something might damage that image—making a mistake, being criticized by the boss, or just not knowing what to do—we feel threatened. We get scared. Our anxiety level begins to go up, and we have to do something to bring it down.

Wired into the oldest part of our brain is a simple solution: Run away and don't come back! The impulse inside all of us is to deal with fear by escaping and developing strategies so we don't have to get close enough to what frightened us to feel afraid again.

This system is quite useful when the things we're afraid of are predatory carnivores. It is best to stay away from them. The trouble is, our brains are wired to handle physical and psychological threats in exactly the same way. Dinosaurs didn't have self-esteem to protect, so evolution never developed a separate system for protecting it. The problem is that *we're* stuck with that same outdated hardware.

When we find ourselves in areas in which threats to

our self-esteem may lurk, we get scared. Our internal warning system says, "Get out of here and stay out! If you hang around here, you're going to make a mistake, get criticized, rejected, or all three. And it's gonna *hurt!*"

Who could blame us for avoiding those areas?

The problem is that physical and psychological threats are different. Psychological threats get bigger the more you run from them. To conquer them, you have to approach them, experience them, learn about them, and see that they aren't so dangerous after all. And all this has to happen while your internal warning system is shrieking like an unattended car alarm. This takes courage, determination, and the guts to admit that fear is the problem.

Admitting to fear, however, is one of those things that makes business people feel incompetent. It is much easier to hop onto the back of a Sacred Bull and head for a shortcut, never considering what the ride costs. Some tough, hard-hitting management types ride this Bull daily.

Afraid? Tony? No way. He takes risks every day that would make your hair turn white. You have to do what it takes to stay competitive in this market. He's in charge of this department and he takes that very seriously.

Making the kinds of deals that keep his department in the black is tricky business. One false move and the game's over. It's Tony's job to see that no one makes a false move. He needs to know everything about everything. If there's a chance you might mess up, you're on the bench and Tony sends himself into the game for you.

There are some who might call that micromanaging, but that's because they don't understand how you play the game for these stakes. All that touchy-feely stuff about empowerment and participatory management are fine for departments that have some leeway. But in a department like

Tony's, only one guy's rear end is on the line, so one guy has to be in control.

This is how Tony explains that he is scared to death to let any of his employees do anything that might make him look bad. It is common fear in business that is usually covered over with this kind of bluster. Trusting the people who work for you is hard and scary. That's why participatory management, empowerment, total quality management, and scores of other power-sharing approaches have such a difficult time getting off the ground.

Managers like Tony get scared if someone else has control of their future, so they clamp down. They cannot admit that they're scared. They rationalize that the job is too complex, too politically sensitive, or too risky to let anyone else call the shots.

Of course, not everyone would agree with this assessment. The guys down in Tony's department think he's kind of power mad for a furnace-room supervisor.

When you are outside the areas you know and understand, your image is in danger. Your automatic impulse is to protect it at all costs. Luckily, you have other areas of the brain that are able to override the reptile's shriek and tell you that we all have to do the things we fear, whether we feel like it or not.

Fear prevents you from confronting psychological dangers. Avoiding what you fear is exactly the *wrong* strategy for dealing with a psychological threat. Actually, you will protect yourself by approaching and learning to cope with whatever task you fear most. Doing the things you don't like or are afraid of is the only way to get ahead. It's also the only way to get the internal feeling of accomplishment that makes you feel as if you're doing something worthwhile with your life. Feeling good about yourself comes less from *how much* you do than from the difficulty of whatever you're doing.

Chasing Away the Bull

We hope this chapter has helped you identify the weird and wonderful strategies people use to avoid the things they don't like to do. When you recognize that you're avoiding something, the battle for change is half won already. The old tricks don't work any more, and you see yourself as avoiding rather than being smarter than the average Bull.

Read the following statements and mark the ones that are true for you. For each statement that you mark true, ask yourself, "Do I go ahead and do it anyway, or do I avoid it?"

1. *I feel rejected when people tell me no.*
2. *I have a hard time relaxing.*
3. *I'm not very good at math.*
4. *It's difficult for me to tell people things that might hurt their feelings.*
5. *I don't like taking risks.*
6. *I feel uncomfortable "blowing my own horn."*
7. *I don't like to work with people who are overly dependent and always need to be told what to do.*
8. *I find it hard to ask for things for myself.*
9. *I have problems with other people telling me what to do.*
10. *I delay telling people things that might make them angry.*
11. *I avoid doing things that are boring.*
12. *It's hard for me to accept criticism.*
13. *I'm not good at playing politics at work.*
14. *I don't like telling people the same things over and over; I expect them to hear me the first time.*
15. *I've been told that I don't have very good "people skills."*
16. *I don't like going to meetings.*

17. *I feel uncomfortable talking in front of groups of people.*

18. *I'm afraid I might be fired if I say how I really feel about things at work.*

19. *I'm not very good at making small talk.*

20. *I'm always behind on my paperwork.*

21. *I'm not a very competitive person.*

22. *I don't believe people should need to be praised for doing what they're supposed to be doing.*

23. *My feelings get hurt fairly easily.*

24. *I have low self-esteem; I don't like myself very much.*

25. *I try to avoid confrontation when I can.*

The above statements are about things people find difficult in their jobs and their lives. We believe that each statement is about skills and actions that are essential for success in your job. If you avoid any of them, your job performance (and the quality of your life) is likely to suffer.

There are real consequences for avoiding any of these skills. Let's consider some of the most common:

- *If you avoid saying things that might upset other people, you may also avoid making tough choices.* (And your employees and coworkers may think you lie.)
- *If you feel uncomfortable "blowing your own horn," you won't "sell" yourself and you won't get ahead.*
- *If you don't like working with people who are overly dependent, you are sidestepping a large part of what management is about.* (If you don't give guidance, direction, and support, what do you do?)
- *If you have problems with people who tell you what to do, your boss probably has problems with you.*
- *If you're not good at playing politics, then someone else will get the interesting job and big raise.*
- *If you're not good at making small talk, the people you work with probably will think you don't like them.*

- *If you don't like going to meetings, too bad.* That's where most of the work that your company thinks is important goes on.
- *If you don't believe in praising people for doing what they're supposed to be doing, you're making do without the most powerful management tool of all.*

If you have convinced yourself that a few of these things are unimportant, you may be in store for feelings of frustration, irritation, disappointment, and emptiness, no matter what Bull you choose to believe.

How to Start Doing What You Don't Like to Do

As you have seen, the Bull of Shortcuts and Blind Spots will try to convince you that you aren't avoiding anything, you're just living by correct priorities. Here are some ideas for cutting through the Sacred Bull and learning to do the things you don't like.

Recognize What You're Avoiding

Compare your priorities with those of successful people in your company or in your field. If your priorities are different, don't automatically assume yours are better.

Kadeem, a social worker, doesn't understand why his peers are so obsessed with documentation and keeping case files up to date. He prides himself on getting out there and really helping people. That's what he was trained for, not filling out stupid forms. He keeps his unfinished charts in cardboard boxes, stacked in the corner of his cubicle. He'll work on them someday when his caseload is low.

Kadeem is avoiding an unpleasant task *and* making a virtue of it. There is a reason why the other social workers are diligent about their paperwork. It's not that they are less dedicated. Instead of drawing his own self-serving conclusions, Kadeem needs to find out why they consider the paperwork so important and how they pace their activities to get it all done.

To recognize what you're avoiding, you also need to pay particular attention to the things you joke about or feel contemptuous of.

Tina is always making jokes about the "Suits" and the silly political games she sees them playing. Whenever she overhears the more political people in her office talking, she'll interrupt with lines like, "Hey, how about letting me in on some of that power schmoozing?"

When somebody treats the boss with anything other than open contempt, Tina makes little kissing sounds. People laugh, so she thinks her jokes are okay. But she does wonder why the Establishment is always dumping on her.

Tina knows very little about the intricacies of office politics. Her ignorance is hiding in her jokes. The problem is that it's hiding from *her.* Everybody else can see it as clearly as a full-page ad in the Sunday paper.

Whenever somebody says, "Employees are our most important investment," or mentions doing things to "empower" people, Colin rolls his eyes and makes jokes. Last week he brought in some love beads and gave them to a manager who frequently mentions empowerment. "Here," Colin said, "I think you should wear these when you talk about this stuff."

Colin doesn't believe in letting employees push him around. He doesn't think any real managers ought to tolerate it.

Colin's jokes hide the fact that he has a few difficulties with new ideas (his management style is circa 1952), as well as with sharing power and trusting the people who work for him.

Identify the Part That Frightens You

Mostly people avoid things they're afraid of. They figure out ways of getting out of situations in which they might look or feel incompetent. Consider the following list to help you identify the part of your job that makes you feel most uncomfortable. This is probably the part you avoid.

- Having to do things differently
- Being a beginner at a task, and being rejected (selling, asking for what you want)
- Having your fate in someone else's hands (sharing power, trusting subordinates)
- Having to do things you see as inconsistent with your personality (promoting yourself, blowing your own horn, being aggressive, standing up for yourself)
- Being bored (Next to looking incompetent, the boredom of paperwork, attention to details, and preparation is what business people fear and avoid most.)

Close the Backdoor

Admit your avoidance strategy to others. Tell people what you're avoiding and how you do it. Most people dread this part because they think that it will make them look foolish or incompetent and that other people will laugh at them. When they try this part of the "change" strategy, however, they are often surprised at how supportive their friends and coworkers can be. To them, you probably looked more foolish when you were blustering and making all those transparent jokes. This Sacred Bull deceives *you* but he doesn't deceive the people around you.

After you have admitted your strategy to other people, give them permission to comment if they see you slipping back into it. You want to close the backdoor and lock it, too.

Kimiko recognizes that she has not been getting the assignments she's wanted because she hasn't been asking for them. She has been through the phase of feeling morally superior because she doesn't play politics or blow her own horn. Now she recognizes that the big thing she's avoiding is being told no. If you ask, you can be turned down. If you don't ask, you can pretend it's an oversight rather than a rejection. Kimiko has been feeling overlooked too long. She realizes it's her own problem, not her boss's.

She explained her insights to three of her closest associates at work, which was hard. She thought they would laugh first at her stupidity, then at her presumption that she was ready for a high-profile assignment. They didn't. Her friends had been wondering all along why she'd been taking herself out of the race. Now they acted as if she'd run a four-minute mile, and high-fived her to loud cheering. Kimiko felt overwhelmed by their encouragement and support, and she appreciated their pledges to keep helping by reminding her to ask for what she wanted.

Have a Plan

Observe or talk with people who are good at the things you are avoiding. How, for example, do successful salespeople handle being told no? How do "detail" people handle the drudgery? Often you'll find that the answers lie in how they talk to themselves about the negative event. "It isn't personal," a top sales rep may say. "All I need to hear is one yes for every hundred nos."

Maybe they set up contingencies for themselves: "Only five more charts and I'll get that cup of coffee." Or, "No socializing until the report is done." Usually their tricks are simple and effective. You can learn them, too, if you ask.

Rehearse Inside Your Head

"Imaginary practice" can help you start doing the things you have been avoiding. You can imagine yourself making a presentation, being calm when talking to a difficult coworker, performing a complicated sequence on the computer, or returning to finish a tedious task no matter how many times you're interrupted.

To make the technique work, be specific about what you will practice. Start with something that you can easily visualize. Use vivid mental pictures of yourself in action. Practice until you can see your action *from beginning to end.*

Practice in the Real World

Do a little every day. Reward small steps in yourself. People who let their fears dictate what they will or won't do may become depressed. Whatever they accomplish doesn't seem like enough. Without challenge, life loses much of its meaning.

When you are scared to death and completely confused, but you do what you need to do anyway, you are chasing away the Sacred Bull. Courage is the ability to make yourself do what you don't want to do when it is what you need to do.

Carlice just knows she doesn't have the right experience. She has worked only in retail sales, and that was years ago. Now she'll be spending her days wearing a headset and sitting in front of a computer console, answering clients' questions about anything and everything her bank does. She must have been crazy to think she could do this. She doesn't know anything about computers. What if she breaks this thing? She doesn't know much about banking either. She gets nervous balancing her own checkbook. Now she has to help hundreds of clients a day balance theirs.

Still, she tells herself, the people who hired her must have thought she was sharp enough. She certainly knows how to be polite to people. And any kid can learn to do math. Carlice sits up straighter and playfully salutes her computer. Whatever it takes, she'll learn it and do it. Whatever it takes.

Josh sat in the office of his newly opened consulting service, waiting for the phone to ring. Potential clients did call, but not nearly enough of them. If business didn't pick up soon, he wouldn't be able to support himself and his family. But he certainly couldn't go out and solicit business, could he? That wouldn't be proper professional behavior. Anyway, if he just did a good job with the clients he had, they would tell other people and soon his client list would expand. Wouldn't it?

Another month of silent phones and sleepless nights sent Josh's rationalization crashing down. He finally admitted that fear was the reason he was trying to build his business by just sitting and waiting for clients. He was scared to do anything else. Fear was stopping him from promoting himself at business gatherings to get leads for consulting contracts. He'd rather be reading in his office than go out and socialize.

Josh decided he would no longer let his fear run his business. If something needed to be done, he would try to do it. First up was the next Chamber of Commerce brunch.

Josh's business has grown; now he's counseling other consultants. He's still a shy person, always gets scared before he speaks to groups. He twists his napkin into tight ropes under the table at business lunches. Many times he has no idea what to say in social situations. But now he says something, *even if he has to stay up late the night before, practicing.*

Chapter Four

THE BULL OF SELF-INTEREST
Look Out for Number One

*T*aurus, Inc., tried to put together a project team with members from six departments to design a new product that would benefit the entire company. Before management could start planning the project, the department heads had to choose the team's players.

"I guess we can give up two people to the team," said Curtis in Engineering. "But, of course, we're going to have to hire two extras to make up for the people we lose to the project. After all, the demand for our services is almost overwhelming as it is."

Curtis knows power and status at Taurus are based on department size and how much of the budget you control. It's a struggle to keep his full-time employees because the kinds of engineers he wants (people with degrees, not the two-year college techs that management is always telling him he should make do with) cost so much. Losing two people would put his department at the same size as Marketing. Those guys already have too much power. Who knows what they do, anyway?

Curtis realizes he could probably get by with a person or two gone for awhile, and this project is the most important thing going on at the moment. It's what the company needs for the future. But he knows it's bad business to suggest that Engineering is anything but overwhelmed with work. If he gives up people now, he may not be able to get them back later on. Better stand firm.

"Well, if Engineering gets two," said Robin in Marketing, "we'll need two extra people, too, to cover our losses to the team."

(I knew it! thought Curtis.) "Oh, give me a break," he said, rolling his eyes. "Why do you need more people? This is what you guys are supposed to be doing in the first place!"

"Excuse me," Robin responded acidly. "Our department has a slate of major, major projects, and this team places a great creative strain on our staff!"

Those engineers! Robin thought. Curtis is a nice guy (mostly), but such an empire builder. He's always attacking Marketing by acting like if you can't express what you're doing in an equation, you're not working. We want strong representation on the project, of course. Our input is essential for success. But I'm not about to give up any FTEs, especially if Engineering is asking for people. Not to ask would look weak!

For most people, the greatest source of frustration and difficulty is the people they work with. Why should this be, particularly when most people are, like you, hardworking and decent, inherently trustworthy and willing to do what's right? Why do people become so difficult when they all work together in a company?

The answer lies in the beliefs people hold unconsciously. Sacred Bulls have a way of telling you that whatever you happen to be doing is the right thing to do. They prevent you from reflecting on your actions and asking yourself if what you are doing is the best way to get what you want. "Just do it," the Bulls say. "Don't think about it."

Nowhere is this more evident in business than in our attitudes about competition and looking out for Number One. The Bull of Self-Interest says, "Go ahead. Look out for yourself first. Everybody else—at least, everybody who is anybody—is doing the same thing."

DISGUISING THE LAW OF THE JUNGLE

This sleek, powerful, and somewhat overfed beast, which equates competitiveness with reflex competition, gives people the idea that competition anywhere, anytime, with anyone, is what business is all about. This is the Bull that says if we all look out for Number One, market forces will look out for us.

We think a Bull this splendid would make excellent hamburger. He can dress up the oldest law on the books—the Law of the Jungle—to look like the latest in management theory. No matter what it says in the corporate mission, the statement of values, or the latest approach to management, when people believe in the Bull of Self-Interest, the real rule is "Look out for Number One. Take care of yourself first because there isn't enough to go around."

For many people, competition with anyone and everyone has become a reflex. This Sacred Bull has turned businesses into jungles, where cooperation makes you easy prey and the only intelligent thing to do is to become a predator.

WHEN COOPERATION TURNS INTO COMPETITION

The idea of competition is so ingrained in business that most people compete all the time, with everyone. They compete because cooperation seems scary or naive. They sacrifice long-term competitiveness for short-term victories and get rewarded by the system for doing so. Most people are so afraid to stop looking out for Number One, even for a minute, that even when they are trying to cooperate they end up competing.

Meanwhile at the Taurus team meeting, other department heads were wondering who would be picking up the tab for support functions for the team.

"That's easy," said Cal in Operations. "This is clearly a Research & Development function. Surely no one expects us to do without people on the line, or donate work space, or strain our tight budget on top of everything we're already contributing to this project. I mean, what's an R&D budget for, anyway?"

Julia, the R&D head, bristled. "Isn't that just typical! Our budget is a pittance! R&D is a companywide function, involvingalldepartments. . . ."

Douglas in Finance couldn't believe what he was hearing. This was supposed to be a team put together using existing resources. He had been adding up a rough total in his head of what people were asking for. It ought to put the company about a million and a half over a budget that's somewhat padded already, he figured.

As much as Taurus needs the new product, we need fiscal restraint more, Douglas thought. Now if he could get in with his accountants and clean up some of the waste in other departments, maybe they could get this special project off the ground.

He figured that the best way was to hold out for no project and see if he could get these people to listen to fiscal reason. He would hate to take the heat for the budget overruns this was going to cause. He'd better go on record now as being against it, in case it turned into a financial disaster.

"This whole idea costs too much," Douglas said flatly. *"Why don't you all just forget this team thing, stick with the product we already have, and improve our profit margin by cleaning up waste in the manufacturing process?"*

The other department heads glared at him.

"By the way," Robin in Marketing said, *"who's in charge here?"*

Curtis in Engineering rolled his eyes again. "We are. Who else? We'll be the guys who end up making this thing fly in the end."

Robin's eyes narrowed. "Is that right? Well, I have some concerns about how . . . appropriate . . . it would be for marketing people to report to an engineer project manager who might not be able to . . . adequately evaluate . . . the creative contribution from other departments."

Cal in Operations agreed. "It would be a lot better for all the team members to report to their respective departments."

"Yes," murmured everyone except Engineering.

As the planning meeting broke up, Curtis turned to the honorary chairman, Bradley, a corporate vice president who had been silent throughout the discussion.

Bradley had been thinking, these people can't get their acts together. They know how important it is to do this project and stay within budget. The future of the company is at stake here, and they're all fighting for power. It's best for me to keep quiet and let them battle it out.

He knew if they came to the wrong decision, he could step in later on. Bradley was looking ahead. All the departments would need downsizing if Taurus was to maintain its competitive position. Moving people into the project would be a convenient place to start. When it's over, he calculated, we can argue convincingly that we don't need so many people. It's best to stand back and let this group decide who's going to get control.

Curtis from Engineering asked, "We can assure our peo-

ple that anybody who works on this project will be guaranteed their former positions when the team's work ends, can't we?"

Bradley shuffled papers.

"Can't we?" Curtis pressed.

The vice president coughed. "Certainly project members would have first pick on anything that comes open as the project is winding down. But it would be . . . imprudent . . . to expect a position guaranteed in this kind of market. Now, if you'll excuse me, I'm late for my next meeting."

What do you think are the chances for this project's success?

No Rewards for Cooperating

The department heads at Taurus are all looking out for themselves. Certainly, they would tell you, nobody else is looking out for their people's interests. That's competition, they would say. It's just the way it is. There are no rewards for cooperating. The department heads believe correctly that their own futures and the future of each department is riding on how tough they can be as negotiators at this table.

The problem is that the future of the whole company is riding on how well project teams like this can develop new products and new ways of doing things in an increasingly competitive market. There is competition out there in the marketplace, but at Taurus everybody is focusing on the internal competition. They have to if they want to keep their jobs.

There are no rewards for collaborating or cooperating, even though that is what is needed to get this project off the ground. The unquestioned rule that the strong survive is making Taurus weaker in the marketplace.

Frustrated, Angry, and Trapped

The department heads at Taurus are decent, well-meaning people. They have the company's best interests at heart. They know they need to cooperate, but they stand to lose if they do. They end up doing what is expected of them—looking out for their own interests, sometimes at the expense of other departments and the company as a whole.

Their own unstated goals—making their departments look good, keeping within their own budgets, and assuring their own staff members' jobs at the end of the project—clash from the beginning with the creative, cooperative behavior the project requires. The department heads know, however, that if they don't look out for themselves, no one else will look out for them.

Inside, Curtis, Robin, Cal, Julia, and Douglas are feeling frustrated, angry, and trapped. They all know that the project cannot accomplish much the way it is set up, but they all feel that they can't back down on their demands. They all go back to their offices with the grim realization that there will be many more battles before this project gets off the ground.

DRAWBACKS OF IN-HOUSE COMPETITION

The usual justification for internal competition is that it improves everyone's performance. Business is like a track meet. You practice racing against your peers, which makes everyone faster. Then, from the results of your internal races, you pick your fastest runners, honed to a competitive edge, to race the competition.

Not only is this an overly simplified view of business, it is an overly simplified view of a track meet as well. It is the view of a rather self-centered runner: Coming in first and his own speed in the big race are the only things that are important. Who cares about his forgotten teammates?

This view can make you believe that the entire purpose of an organization is to support the personal competition of a few talented senior managers. The forgotten people feel used and resentful (and the other managers begin to think that they need new track shoes—it must be the shoes!).

A track meet may be business, but business is not a track meet. Business involves complex organization, teamwork, trust, and sustained, long-term effort. Internal competition may make a few already-fast people faster, but it gets in the way of many other things that are just as important.

As we see it, internal competition has three major problems:

1. *Internal competition leads to a mental division of the company into "players" and "nobodies."* Even though the nobodies are necessary for the success of the business, they are often unconsciously excluded from whatever is going on.

2. *Instead of rewarding the people who do the best job, internal competition rewards those who are best at manipulating the system.*

3. *Internal competition fosters a climate of fear and distrust that inhibits performance and undermines competitive position.*

PLAYERS AND NOBODIES

As we discussed in our previous book, *Neanderthals at Work* (Wiley, 1992), every business is made up of three cultures: Rebels, the people who are creative, good in a crisis, but don't like to be told what to do; Believers, who think if you work hard and play by the rules you'll get ahead (or at least get rewarded); and Competitors, who understand politics and how to use it to accomplish their goals.

Of the three groups, the Competitors tend to move into management, where they set up systems that work fine for Competitors but leave the other two groups feeling excluded.

Competitors are good at figuring out what the real rules are in any system without being told. They often set up systems in which there are rules that exist for show, but the real rules—how to get ahead—are never spoken. Competitors believe in self-selection. You have to demonstrate you have what it takes by showing you can figure out for yourself what is really important.

No matter what business or profession you're in, your success will be largely determined by your ability to perceive and live by rules that nobody ever tells you.

This results in a tremendous waste of human resources as well as feelings of elitism, which can often lead people unconsciously to set up companies that are structured upside down. In such a company, your major job responsibility is to make your boss look good rather than to see that the people below you have what they need in materials and instruction to do a good job. The major rewards come for achieving rank rather than for doing a good job. (As you will see in the next section, these may be very different sets of behaviors.) Once people achieve rank, their unconscious ideas about what their privileges should be can get in the way of their responsibilities.

"PRINCE CHARLES"

Charles is the senior vice president who heads up the entire Western Region. To the people in the various divisions in Western, his position seems largely ceremonial, consisting of state visits for which everything is cleaned up beyond recognition.

A few select managers get to kiss his ring (other parts of the anatomy have been mentioned by the less reverent) and give reports and input. All is carefully staged to show that this division is running quite well, thank you, and needs no special attention from above. "Special attention" usually takes the form of reorganization, in which a few upper-level managers are removed. ("If you can't do it, we'll have to put in someone who can.")

Western Region usually prides itself on its austerity and fiscal responsibility. When Charles comes, all meetings are catered by the best restaurant in town. Coffee is poured into bone china from silver pots. The rest of the time, even managers are expected to wash their own mugs.

Last year Western had to lay off nine people. The savings realized came to about half of Charles's annual salary.

To most employees, Charles is the kind of person whom the peasants would have cheerfully sent to the guillotine in the French Revolution. Most of us, from our view below, are accustomed to seeing people like him resentfully. But let's look at how things appear to Charles.

The View from the Top

To Charles, his major work is in the boardroom back at headquarters. Being in charge of Western Region is just his ticket of admission. He appoints managers to run the operation, and he leaves them alone as long as their numbers are good. If they aren't, well, that's what reorganizations are for.

Charles sees his salary, perks, and privileges as vital motivations that keep the system going. The regional vice presidents all know that if they play their cards right (beat out their peers) they will have a shot at a senior position. There has to be some reward for excellence, otherwise the people below him (the ones who have what it takes, anyway) won't be motivated to compete for a position like his. Charles regards this competition as the engine that runs the whole organization.

To tell the truth, Charles is a little uncomfortable with all the ceremony and deference. Underneath, he's just an ordinary kind of guy. And the salary—well, most of that goes in taxes. Most of the perks are symbols really, incentives to get other people to do their best and a signal to other companies with whom Charles has to deal that he is every bit as important as they are.

Charles's real work is in the boardroom at headquarters. He will tell you there is no preference shown there. The competition is stiff and constant. Every word must be analyzed for nuances about which way the winds of power might be blowing. The board has no reputation for mercy, and only the strong survive. The demands are tremendous.

The money and privileges, in his mind, are reasonable for the amount of pressure he has to live with every day. This is how a major corporation is run, and you won't catch Charles whining about it.

The system at Charles's company is based on tough competition from top to bottom. The winners get their rewards and the losers get, well, what losers get. To Charles and the upper managers, this system makes a lot of sense because they believe market forces look after those who look out for themselves.

Let's look at the kind of system they have unconsciously created.

Doing the Work Has Low Status

Charles and his peers dismiss the resentment of the rank and file, chalking it up to naiveté or authority issues and, as such, of little importance. Charles's behavior sets the standard for all the other managers in the region. These managers are Competitors. They don't have to be told what is important. They look to the behavior of the people above them to know what counts. They recognize that the culture of the company demands that people be very aware of the appropriate tasks for their ranks.

Charles's real job is dealing with the CEO and the board. The division managers have to please Charles to keep their jobs, as their managers have to please them. Management style is to encourage competition to get to the next highest level.

Successful people learn quickly that the rewards come for spending most of your time with people above you, or at least with peers. People who spend too much time with those below them are not doing their job.

This pushes the actual production of goods and services and (heaven forbid) dealing with customers down to the lowest level of status. Like stable slopping and waiting on tables, this work is considered unimportant. If you know what's what, you'll get away from it as quickly as you can.

This is also true of spending too much time seeing that your subordinates know what they're supposed to be doing and have what they need to do it. If they have what it takes, they'll handle it themselves.

Actually doing the work is the fate of people who don't have the guts and motivation to be players in the competitive game that is the real culture of the company. It is very difficult to take pride in doing the day-to-day work when you keep getting messages that this is not what your company really values.

"This Is Who We Are"

This is not the system the management of Charles's company had planned. In fact, they would vehemently deny that this is the way it is. They would point to the values statement or the TQM program and say, "This is who we are." They aren't lying either (although they may be slinging a bit of Bull). They really believe that competition and rewards for beating out the other guy are the way to get high-level production and quality.

The entire system is the unconscious result of believing that business is based on competition and competition is based on looking out for Number One.

Competing with anyone and everyone is a reflex you have to develop if you are to be seen as fit for any but the most unimportant work. If you don't compete, you're a nobody. The choice is up to you.

At all levels of companies like Charles's, people feel pulled to choose between doing what it takes to do a good job and doing what it takes to get ahead. In some workplaces, these behaviors bear very little resemblance to each other.

It is this dilemma that causes the most internal conflict and stress for reflective, intelligent, and basically decent managers. Like most people in business, they really want to do a good job for the companies that employ them. All around them, however, they see the biggest rewards going to people who know how to manipulate the system to their own advantage.

SHARK IN A BROOKS BROTHERS SUIT

Jack is a bright, ambitious guy on the fast track of his industry. He knows he can make division head in the next five years. After that, who can tell? CEO isn't out of the question.

Jack's strategy involves moving from one job to another, from company to company, always upward. His tactics are similar wherever he goes: Move in, get expenses in line and, when the bottom line looks good, move on to the next job.

Jack has built himself quite a reputation as the kind of guy who can turn a department around in nothing flat. Here's how he does it:

As soon as he gets hired, he meets with his lower-level managers and tells them, "Not all of you will be here three months from now." This gets their attention. He pauses for a long time, knowing that inside their heads they're waiting for the next word, the one that will tell them what they have to do to keep their jobs. He knows from experience that the longer he waits and the more offhandedly he says it, the more impact it has.

"Expenses." He doesn't even have to finish the sentence. He just shakes his head. A word to the wise is sufficient.

Jack believes that performance can always be improved by fear, confusion, and competition. He believes people who are too comfortable will not be motivated enough to do their best work. He thinks people need to work scared, or they will hold back and coast. Jack's after more than an improvement in performance. He wants spectacular numbers for the kind of turnaround that will add to his legend.

This is enough for the first week. This will get the managers back to their departments, looking closely at their balance sheets, and figuring what they can cut to make their bottom lines look good enough.

The problem is, after the initial cuts, the managers start getting together, making deals, and coming to agreements about what services, positions, and expenditures are essential and should not be cut. They figure solidarity is their best defense. They will push and prod each other to cut what they think is reasonable, and they will present Jack with what they think is a reasonable plan that they can all agree on. This, Jack knows, will cut a few percentage points. A good start, but not nearly enough.

If Jack stopped here, he might improve the department's performance over the long haul, getting the managers to work together out of fear of external consequences. Jack, however, has no intention of stopping here. He is just getting started.

Jack needs to up the ante. His next step is usually to fire two people. From experience he has learned that it doesn't much matter who goes. The purpose of the firings is to show that he is in control and means business, and to raise the general anxiety level. What he wants the managers to feel, actually, is "the next one could be me." This stimulates their creativity.

While things are bubbling and boiling, and the confused managers are trying to figure out why those particular people got the axe, Jack will move on to the second phase. He will use one of the vacancies to bring in his own chosen Number Two.

Clarisse has been with him in the past two jobs. Jack's specialty is finance. Clarisse is a wizard with PR. They both know that, with disruptions coming in the department, information must be carefully managed. Clarisse writes the material for the presentations Jack makes to upper management about how expenses are dropping and quality and morale are improving.

Some frightened managers will be willing to toe this party line if they see in it the means of their salvation. Jack and Clarisse reframe the rest of the managers as people who are stuck in the old ways of thinking, concerned with their own areas but unable to buy into the new vision of efficiency that is "essential to maintaining a competitive position in the global marketplace" (read that as "these guys are dogmeat").

This is a neat trick—casting the people who are concerned enough to say, "Hey, wait a minute; there are some problems with what's going on here," as selfish, and the ones who have become complete toadies as "team players who want what's best for the whole department." It usually works.

Jack replaces the recalcitrant managers with "acting managers" at a much lower salary. The implicit promise is that if they "work out," the job is theirs to keep.

Expenses go down even further. The remaining managers—especially the acting managers, bless their hearts; they're so motivated—are working around the clock to keep production up. All the while they're telling everyone how great things are in the department. Even if one or two employees break ranks and complain, who will listen? From the outside, the department is the picture of health and efficiency.

Jack is great at keeping things in balance for as long as it takes to find a new job. He usually grooms a successor (*sacrificial lamb* is really a more accurate term) from inside. This is the guy who will take the fall when everything comes apart as soon as Jack leaves.

The people to whom Jack reports may say the only mistake Jack made was thinking Willis had what it took to head up the department. By this time, though, Jack is long gone—either up a level or two in this company or in another one.

THE GOLDEN BOY STRIKES AGAIN

Jack is quite a disturbed human being, most readers (and psychologists) would agree. He shamelessly uses other people to accomplish his own ends. He leaves a department behind that is gutted and demoralized. He does it all with a winning smile, a firm handshake, and world-class audiovisuals (courtesy of Clarisse). People like Jack thrive in an environment where competition means looking out for Number One. He is Number One.

People as disturbed as Jack are relatively rare. If you have one as a boss, you can do little to protect yourself individually. The only way the department could have defended itself was by pulling together and recognizing Jack's game before he was fully in control. Jack takes on departments that are in trouble already, so the chance of their organizing opposition to him is almost nil. Jack holds all the cards, and that's the only way he'll play.

The best we can do about the Jacks of the world is to take a very close look at the conditions under which they flourish—the very conditions set up by the Bull of Self-Interest. One day maybe he'll go too far and get indicted or perhaps go into politics, where he will find out how real sharks play the game.

Our concern is with the serious and decent managers who see how well the competitive system rewards people like Jack. These managers face having to choose between their principles and their jobs. Take it from us. Whatever you feel now, you don't know what choice you would make until you're put in the position.

Ned, fifty-five years old and the father of two kids in college, is a manager in Jack's department. He needs a job that pays a decent salary and is afraid he couldn't get one anywhere else. Ned believes that Jack's demands on his department are impossible. But Jack is so relentless that, if he knew what was really going on, he would fire Ned on the spot. Luckily, Jack won't find out what's really going on. Ned has devised dozens of little ways to cook the books and doctor the numbers so that his department looks great on paper.

Some of the things he's doing are downright dishonest. Luckily, he knows the system well enough to conceal his manipulations, but sometimes he snaps awake in the middle of the night, sweating. Someday, somehow, someone may find out. Ned doesn't like having to operate this way. He doesn't have the same stomach for this kind of behavior that Jack does. But Jack is calling the tune, and Ned has to dance or get out. He doesn't want to do things this way, but he feels he doesn't have any choice. It's a tough world out there. His family needs his paycheck; they're counting on him. Ned is just looking out for Number One.

Michelle, another manager in Jack's department, would never dream of altering the books. She just passes along Jack's management style and lets her employees deal with it. They do deal with it, by competing among themselves to keep sales up and costs down. In a competitive system like this, you have to beat somebody.

Eventually people go after customers, who are easy targets in the short run. Michelle's managers make their quotas by pushing shoddy merchandise out the door, overselling parts in repairs, and overcharging for just about everything. Michelle knows that these practices are going on, but she doesn't ask too many questions. She follows another Sacred Bull: "What she doesn't see isn't there."

All of the people in our examples thus far (except Jack) are basically decent and hardworking. They are people like you. Some are engaged in illegal and unethical behavior. All are involved in doing things that are best for themselves but damaging for their company.

"Prince Charles" doesn't recognize the effect his privilege has on the other people in the company. Everyone else feels caught up in a system they didn't create. They do what they do not because they are basically bad or dishonest but because they are terrified of losing their jobs. The only person who is not actually breaking the rules or covering up the broken rules is Jack. So who is responsible?

Psychologists will tell you that normal, decent people are capable of doing terrible things if they are frightened enough or believe that someone in authority is telling them to go ahead. None of us knows for sure what we would do under sufficient pressure. Psychologists will also tell you that a little anxiety will improve performance. The effects drop off very quickly, however. Terror doesn't improve anything.

Jack's strategy of keeping people in a state bordering on panic leads to desperate behavior. Jack would say, "If they can't handle the competition, they ought to get out of the game." He is, of course, an extreme example. However, similar situations actually happen, even in "nice" companies that do not question the notion that competition is the driving force behind every action.

This Bull Breeds Fear and Distrust

The worst thing about the Bull of Self-Interest is not the monsters he creates but what he does to regular people. For people who follow the "Look out for Number One" rule, competition becomes a reflex. People don't think about it; they just do it. They confuse reflex, or automatic, competition with effective competitiveness.

Competitiveness is the result of cooperation. A whole company that is working together in a coordinated way is much more effective than a bunch of people who are all out for themselves.

We are not saying that the typical person in an internally competitive environment will try to take advantage of other people or of the company. Most of us will try to do the best we can. The problem comes from all the things we have to do to keep other people from taking advantage of us.

In an environment with a lot of internal competition, there is always a high background level of fear and distrust that gets in the way of working together.

Stuart has come to Dean, his boss, with an idea that, if handled right, might make the company a little money. With some modifications, one of their products might meet the needs of several high-tech firms in the area. Stuart has some contacts, and he has done a little advance work. Now he's asking for a small team from Design and Manufacturing and a chance to make it happen.

Dean sees some merit in the idea, but it's a big financial risk. Too big. He could put together the team, but it would be a drain on his budget. Earnings this quarter are not that solid. It would be at least three quarters before the project would bring in any money, and all that time Dean's department would have to support it even though other departments would share in the profits. Dean bears the risk, but the other guys get just as much of the gain.

Dean could bring up the idea at the management meeting, but that would bring in Marketing and Sales. They'd put in a pittance and demand total control. Any benefits would have to be divided with them for their "help" (like coming in and taking over the operation because they figure he's not smart enough to do it himself). If the idea took off, they'd demand a bigger share of the gains.

If Dean proposes it, his boss will be riding him for results. No, Dean can't see enough gain for him to warrant bringing it up with the other managers. Once he does, it's out of his hands.

So Dean goes back to Stuart and says, "Sorry, Stu, this just isn't a good time for new projects. You know how conservative the management team is. But, hey, keep those ideas coming. They're what makes this company great!"

Two years later, when the competition makes a bundle on a similar idea, Dean's boss shakes his head and says, "I wish we'd thought of that."

Well, Dean tells himself, it wasn't exactly *the same idea anyway. Who knows if it would have worked as well? It's just lucky Stuart got another job so there's nobody around to start a chorus of "I told you so."*

An atmosphere of such intense internal competition may drive away talented, competent people in the number-two spot within a department. Like Stuart, they may choose to leave a company rather than continue fighting the internal system. Their absence creates a gap in competence and authority between the person at the top and the subordinates below the vacated number-two spot. Filling the spot may not replace the valuable voice calling for real competitiveness through cooperation.

In the real world, as in the example, reflex competition manifests itself in subtle ways through the management of information: The best way to look out for Number One is to be very careful about what you tell people. You have to carefully weigh the possible losses to yourself before you tell other people things that may benefit them. This is true of suggesting ideas that might make money. It is even more true of offering your opinion.

"Kicking around ideas" is one of the major jobs of most management teams. The process sounds casual and open, but the skill and subtlety involved in this kind of kicking can rival what you see in World Cup soccer.

"Kick It Around"—Carefully

Phil has a new idea. He's researched it six ways from Sunday and is pretty sure it will fly. He's also very sure that if he brings it up, Lou and Carol will automatically shoot it down because it's his idea. They are not about to let him score a point.

Phil knows that the two of them can easily stomp anything into the dirt. It's always much easier to criticize someone else's idea than to come up with one of your own. (Phil knows; he's gunned down a few brainstorms himself.)

To get his idea to fly, Phil has to be subtle.

Maybe somebody else could bring up a vague, half-baked version with lots of flaws—somebody Lou and Carol hate. Larry's a perfect choice. He's owed Carol one for awhile, and everybody knows Lou thinks Larry's an idiot. (To tell the truth, Larry really isn't all that bright. He's perfect for this.)

Phil will prime Larry with a flawed version of the idea. He'll mention how it will take Carol by surprise and make her look like she hasn't done her homework. Lou and Carol will go after Larry and decimate his idea. They'll use all their best arguments on the inferior version, and that will give Phil a chance to prepare for their criticisms.

Just when Lou and Carol are sure they've stomped it flat, Phil will say, in his patented, offhand way, "Lou and Carol have some good points. But, you know, if we do it this way, we can get around most of the major pitfalls they have so astutely raised." Then the field is clear, and he can run the idea all the way to the goal. Yeah, it'll work.

Phil picks up his phone. "So, Larry, what are you doing for lunch today?"

Operating this way is so much a part of business that we seldom consider any alternatives. Too dangerous. Ineffective. Stupid. Nor do we think too much about why we do things like this. Maddening, destructive, and inefficient as it is, we all accept internal competition as a fact of life. "Take care of yourself; nobody else will take care of you." Like all the other beliefs that make up Sacred

Bull, we don't talk about it; we seldom think about it. We just live by it.

Maintaining Internal Competition

Just as people accomplish most competition by managing information, they can also maintain the feeling of internal competition by what they say and don't say:

"Our expenses are out of line."
"This is a highly competitive industry."
"Some downsizing is going to be necessary in some departments."
"Some people won't be able to cut it."
"The employment-for-life mentality is dead."

All of these statements are true of many companies in these economic times. We know and accept them as facts. We say them all the time. But think about how you would feel about these statements if your boss began a meeting with even one or two of them. Your heart would pound. Your breath would catch in your throat. You would start wondering who goes and who stays. You might start calculating and realize that the people who keep their jobs are the ones who play the system best. As you calculate, your coworkers would be doing some figuring, too. Each of you would be thinking *not* "What's best for the company?" but "How am I going to keep my job?"

You could be putting your skills to better use, don't you think? We think so, too. Fear can be an effective motivator in small doses, but it is so easy to use that managers often do it without considering the effects of overuse. In a similar way, occasional internal competition can bring out the best in people but, as a steady diet, it more often brings out the worse.

Some people handle internal competition better than others. Most manage it by developing their own rules to live by that minimize the danger they perceive. The rules most people live by in an internally competitive environment are not "Work harder and come up with new ideas and you'll get ahead." They are closer to the following:

"Keep your head down."
"Don't spend any money."
"Make the other guy look bad."
"Negotiate for tasks below what you know you can do."
"Attach yourself to somebody powerful and do everything he or she says."
"Keep your mouth shut."

These are not the attitudes that make a company competitive in the marketplace. These are the attitudes of frightened and desperate people, which are precisely what the Bull of Self-Interest leaves in its wake.

WHAT TO DO ABOUT INTERNAL COMPETITION

In much of what we write, we offer lists of things you can do about difficult situations. With internal competition, this is not so easy. As you have seen in this chapter, internal competition is powerful and pervasive, and so much a part of our way of doing things that we seldom think about it.

Not thinking about it really is the part that is psychologically most damaging. One of the most important elements necessary for psychological health is a feeling of control over your own life. Most of us work in environments in which the amount of internal competition is a source of stress that is mostly beyond our control.

We won't insult you by saying that if you cooperate, the world will cooperate with you and a newer, kinder era of competitiveness will miraculously zap into existence. You know as well as we do that there are very few rewards out there for cooperating, especially in the short run.

There are some things you can do, however. As with anything done by Sacred Bulls, internal competition works best when nobody pays attention. Pay attention. It is easy to see all the destructive, lying, backbiting types of behavior people use. More difficult to see is the philosophy behind it. They are looking out for Number One because they think that is the correct way to do things. This is the part nobody thinks about.

Thinking about it is the first step. Talk about internal competition. Bring it up in meetings. Of course, this can be dangerous. It is always easier to see and point out what other people are doing to make your office destructively competitive; it is much more difficult to see what you do. It feels as if you are just reacting in the only way possible.

KEEPING DOWN THE DAMAGE THIS BULL CAN DO

The Bull of Self-Interest does his worst damage when people follow him without being aware that there is any other direction to go. The key to limiting his damage is to make competition a choice rather than a reflex.

As an Organization

There are several options for controlling damage in an organization.

1. *Decide what's best for business.* As you begin a project or activity, decide each time what is best for business in this case. Should people compete with each other or cooperate to get this particular job done?

If you are competing, what would you be doing? What would you be thinking? How would you know you were in competition with each other instead of in cooperation? It is important that you actually talk about the thoughts and behaviors that make up competition because so many people just do them without thinking.

A good starting point is to talk about holding back information and opinions. Ask the group if there are things they feel they can't say. (Let them respond anonymously on paper if you don't want to be told only what you want to hear.)

The group can help set the accepted level of competition. If the group sees internal competition as getting in the way, instead of as a form of political savvy, everyone will take a step toward cooperation.

2. *Discuss what is rewarded.* What does it take to get ahead in your work group or company? Can you get ahead by taking advantage of your peers or subordinates? How would anybody know? What are the available rewards in this system—promotions, good assignments, bonuses, respect? To whom do they go and for what behavior?

Are individuals or groups rewarded? When something good happens, does the manager get the reward or does the whole group benefit? If only the manager stands to be rewarded for good group performance, the stage is set for getting ahead at other people's expense.

Make an honest assessment of where things stand. All Sacred Bulls thrive best under a thick cover of platitudes. You must be able to go beyond saying "Everything's great now, and we can become even greater." If you cannot discuss negative or embarrassing information, no changes are possible.

3. *Ask the people who work with your stars.* Competitors excel at making the view from above look great.

Check some of the other views before assigning star status to particular people. See how their peers, subordinates, and even customers evaluate them. Make the evaluations anonymous and make them count. You may not get specifics, but you will get clues if something is going wrong. Maybe your "star" is generating wonderful numbers at the company's expense, taking advantage of other people, overselling, or even pushing shoddy merchandise. You will have to check out what you hear, of course, or this kind of evaluation is not worth doing.

As an Individual

Awareness is the key to limiting the damage from the Bull of Self-Interest. It is always easy to point to other people who abuse the system. The hard part is recognizing what you are doing to maintain the atmosphere of internal competition.

1. *Ask yourself who are your main rivals.* Start by asking who seems to be competing with you (or taking advantage of you). Try to figure out what game they're playing. What are the rules? What do they get if they win?

Then ask yourself how you are playing the same game. If your answer is, "I'm just not playing," you need to analyze yourself a little more deeply. The Bull of Denial may be standing in your way. In the competition game, you can't *not* play. If you think you're not playing, it usually means you are relying on someone else to play for you. Or you may not be seeing yourself as others see you. We all compete. The question is, how?

2. *Look at what you keep secret.* Most destructive competition involves deception or, at least, obfuscation. What are the things you don't tell people? Why can't you tell them? Withholding information from someone is a clue that you are in competition with that person. We are not suggesting you tell everybody everything. Just be very aware of the editing you're doing and why you're doing it. What would happen if they knew? If you are honest with yourself, what you're holding back contains the elements of your strategy. For example:

"I can't tell employees that there are other funds to cover equipment or overtime. If they knew, they'd run up the budget."
"My salary isn't anybody's business."
"I can't tell my boss that my quota is a little low, that I can make it without even breaking a sweat. I have to make her think it's harder than it is."
"Central office can't find out that we have some dissatisfied customers here."

You have choices about your own behavior. It's up to you to decide what's best for you personally. Is the way you're playing the game making it harder for you to get cooperation when you need it?

3. *Assume that everyone is your customer.* The most important alliance you can make is with your customers. To develop a broader definition of *customer*, think about what you supply that other people want. Recognize that everyone is your customer: your boss, your coworkers, and the people you manage.

Start with your boss; that's usually the easiest. But then keep going—to your employees, your coworkers, your clients, even your family and friends. What do you give them? What else do they need from you? How can you find out what they need? What did you do or say that produced the most cooperation? Which behavior resulted in more conflict and less cooperation? What can you do to raise the cooperation level? If you're still not sure what people need from you, *ask*.

Chapter Five

THE BULL OF MIND READING
People Should Know
Without Being Told

Ten managers report to Marcus, and he wonders why they can't all be like Kristen and Doug. Not that these two are perfect, but they both seem to make the extra effort to figure out what's going on. They're awake, and Marcus's other managers seem half-asleep.

Last week, for instance, the executive VP came out from headquarters for a visit. Any rookie manager should have realized what the VP wanted to see (what Marcus wanted him to see): a smooth-running operation with happy employees, happy managers, the flag of motivation flying, and Marcus at the helm of a taut, efficient ship. Was that too much to ask?

Instead, when the VP sat down with the managers and asked if anybody wanted to "share a problem," only Kristen and Doug had the basic smarts to figure out the right answer: No problems here; everything's under control. All the other managers used the meeting to wash dirty laundry in front of the number-two man in the entire company.

Later it took Marcus two hours to explain that his divi-

sion, rather than being a hotbed of unrest and low morale, was really full of managers who were so dedicated that they just couldn't rest until every little problem was solved. It took some big-time spin-doctoring to put that one across.

What could those people have been thinking? Did they have to be told that this was a state visit and their job was to present their best image to the VP? Kristen and Doug recognized that, of course. They put on a show that did the whole division proud. Marcus just wished that all his managers were as motivated as those two. It would certainly make his life easier.

The Bull of Mind Reading will tell you that if people have the right feelings on the inside, they will do the right things on the outside. If people are motivated, have the proper work ethic, or really care about their employees, they won't have to be told what to do. They will know already.

Many managers believe that this Sacred Bull has magical powers. They point as evidence to the handful of people in their department who do their jobs well without needing detailed instructions. "See?" these managers say. "At least I'm getting through to some people. At least *they* get it. But what's wrong with the rest of them?"

The Bull of Mind Reading lies at the root of the disappointment and distrust that often exists between managers and their employees. Relying on mind reading as a management style leaves managers feeling impatient and irritated with the employees who need more specific information to perform at top capacity. In turn, the employees sense they have disappointed the boss, but usually have no idea what they need to do to meet expectations. After all, they aren't mind readers.

THE BULL'S TOP 20 PERCENT

Marcus thought he was seeing evidence of superior motivation. What he was really seeing is evidence of a fact well known to psychologists—that virtually all skills and abilities are distributed along a normal curve. Twenty percent of the group will be superior performers; 60 percent, average; and 20 percent, below average.

What Marcus was really seeing was that Kristen and Doug were at the top end of the normal curve for *observational learning*. This is the learning people do by watching successful people and imitating what they do, without being explicitly told. Studies show that about 20 percent of any group of employees will be good enough at learning by observation to figure out what is expected. These employees need minimal direction, little support, and no checking on. Like Kristen and Doug, they don't need much management because they seem to know how to manage themselves.

Bosses see these top 20 percent performers and wonder, often with irritation, "Why can't the rest of my department figure out what it takes?" The Bull of Mind Reading persuades them to expect the same ability from the other 80 percent, usually with frustrating results for both sides.

WHY MANAGERS AND EMPLOYEES FEEL FRUSTRATED

Managers are frustrated because they mistake ability for motivation. Intelligent people often just assume that other people are as intelligent as they are. They think everybody knows what they know and can do what they can do. They might think of people who can't as stupid, but more often they will see them as lacking in motivation.

These managers don't think of themselves as in the top

20 percent of abilities. More often they think of themselves as willing to do the hard work that it takes to get
the job done. They think they are successful because of
their superior motivation, not because things come more
easily to them.

Imagine the frustration of feeling that 80 percent of
the people you manage could do what you can if they
were just willing to make the effort.

We are not saying here that managers are frustrated
because they are smart and their employees are dense.
The situation can be just as frustrating when it is the
other way around.

Most of us assume that other people think the way we
think and know what we know. When we know something, it seems so obvious that we forget how it felt or
what we thought when we didn't know it. To people who
don't know exactly what we know in the way that we know
it, we seem to be expecting them to be mind readers.

The problem becomes more perplexing as we look
more closely. Kristen and Doug in the preceding example
watched their boss, Marcus, and did what he did. What
they saw, however, was different from what their colleagues who were less skillful observed. Kristen and
Doug saw Marcus doing everything he could to make a
good impression on the VP, and they noticed that part
of his act was to downplay problems.

The other managers also noticed Marcus trying to
make a good impression, but they assumed that the way
to impress the VP was to give him the information he
asked for. After all, they had seen Marcus giving him
information many times throughout his visit. However,
they did not notice that the information Marcus was
giving was only positive. These managers were just as
motivated as Kristen and Doug, but they were not as
skillful at figuring out which behaviors to imitate.

We tend to think of learning the skills of our job as
building up an ever-enlarging collection of facts. This is

not actually what happens at all. The facts come very early in the learning process. Increases in skill do not come from an increase in the store of facts in your head but in the ability to make finer and finer discriminations.

Suppose you were to look at two diamonds of about the same size. Chances are you wouldn't be able to tell which was the more valuable even if the difference in value was in the thousands of dollars. Show the two diamonds to an experienced jeweler, however, and he wouldn't even have to put the loupe in his eye to know which was more valuable.

The jeweler might point out subtle differences in color, minute fractures, and wispy inclusions, but these variations would surely be hard for you to see even after you are told what they're supposed to look like. Yet they make all the difference in the worth of a stone. To the jeweler, your difficulty would seem ridiculous. He *told* you what to look at. It's as obvious to him as a billboard. He might conclude that you are either hopelessly stupid or unwilling to make the effort to see what is right in front of you.

If you have ever been in a situation like this, it's very easy to see why employees get frustrated. They may be highly motivated and intelligent, but if they don't know precisely what to look for, they may be seen as unmotivated, stupid, or lazy.

Managers get frustrated because they think learning job skills is a matter of amassing facts. All of their employees know the basics. They may even have degrees in the subject. So, the manager thinks, why can't they do the job as well as I can? The answer is, they don't see the facts the way you do.

Most managers are good at *doing*. They may not be particularly skilled at analyzing what they do and explaining it to other people. The Bull of Blind Spots ("What I don't like can't be important") will tell them that's what *teachers* are supposed to do—not managers. Actually the best managers have many of the skills of good teachers. Teachers assume that students don't know what the teacher knows and that the main purpose of teaching is to get them to understand the subject as well as the teacher does. The Bull of Mind Reading can convince managers that they aren't there to teach but to get the job done.

"SEE? THEY GET IT"

The Bull will point to the 20 percent who "get it" and use them as evidence of the success of your management style on the people who are motivated enough to listen. What you're actually seeing, however, is the innate abilities of the top 20 percent, who don't need managing at all.

These people are skilled enough at the job and at observational learning to read your mind. They can give you what you want with very little direction. They can read the subtle nuances of your behavior and, from them, figure out what you require of them. In short, you don't have to manage them; *they* can manage *you*. The frustrating part of managing is dealing with the other 80 percent who do need some managing. It's much easier when people can read your mind.

For employees, the frustration comes from being valued based on what seems, to them, to be their ability to read minds. Why, then, don't we just tell the people who work for us what we want? It isn't that easy. What we want is for people to do things the way we would do them. Aside from the sheer complexity of explaining what to do besides knowing procedure, we also want them to exercise judgment—to know as we do when to deviate from the standard procedure.

Usually in Marcus's department if someone asks for information, standard procedure is to give it. Marcus would prefer that certain kinds of information be withheld or glossed over in front of the vice president—unless, of course, the VP asks directly, in which case you don't lie.

But what if the VP asks, "Are there any problems?" and you think there are some. The answer depends on what kind of problems—some kinds the department just has to deal with on its own. The VP is not really interested, and mentioning them just sounds petty or as if you don't know what you're doing.

"So," people ask, "we're supposed to cover up?"

Well, not exactly cover up.

As Marcus discovered, organizational politics and getting along with people can be sticky. Organizational politics involves making some very fine discriminations indeed. It is very difficult, and sometimes embarrassing, to specify exactly what you want people to do—especially if they don't quite understand your meaning and then go on to explain what you said to someone else.

Sometimes it sounds as if you really ought not to be asking people to do the kinds of things they have to do to make the department, the company, themselves—and you—look good. It's not that these things are immoral. It's just that they lie outside of what we usually think of as job requirements.

For example, we have never seen a job description that explicitly said, "Please your boss." How are people supposed to know that this is a critical part of any job? The Bull of Mind Reading will say employees are just supposed to know it. But what if they don't?

Worse, people are often given incorrect or incomplete information and expected to know exactly what to disregard and when. Twenty percent will know; the other 80 percent will be confused, frustrated, and ultimately inefficient.

American Excellence & Quality (AEQ) always had the latest in management programs. They were the first to exper-

iment with quality circles in the early '80s. They have TQM and empowerment now. Those programs are nice, but the people who know have always seen them as window dressing. It's production that everyone really pays attention to.

Production determines what happens to you: whether you get bonuses, promoted, or laid off. Production is what AEQ is all about. The people who are good at observational learning learn that you talk about quality and empowerment but you keep your production up, no matter what it takes.

AEQ is not an unusual environment. All companies have programs and procedures that are more for show than for real use. To really get ahead, you have to be able to figure out what to pay attention to and what to ignore. This is very hard for managers to explain, so in many cases you have to get it by mind reading. You should know without being told.

WHY SHOULD YOU LEARN MIND READING?

Your future depends on how well you are able to learn the things nobody ever tells you. Mind reading is a survival skill.

Even though your company expects you to know many things without being told, you can't expect the decision makers to know without being told what a valuable employee you are. They have to be told in a way that they can hear, even if it's completely obvious to you. Play the Downsizing Paranoia game to find out what we mean.

The Downsizing Paranoia Game

Most people see layoffs and downsizing as totally outside their control. They rely on mind reading by management to protect them. The Sacred Bull particularly likes to play this game with people who think their jobs are safe because management "just knows" how valuable they are to the company. These people do not see that, unless they work in a very small company, the person who decides the fate of their jobs will *not* know what good workers they are.

Downsizing Paranoia is a game for people who stay up late worrying about their job security. Any number can play. The game goes like this.

Pretend you are the division head or chief of the Fiscal Department and you have to make layoffs. Get a sheet of paper and divide it down the middle. Write Go *on one side and* Stay *on the other.*

Think of the people in your department, including yourself. Try to figure out what decision management would make about each person and why. Look at the department next door, too. (The most common downsizing strategy is to combine several departments and get rid of a manager or two.)

Now make your list.

How did you decide who stays and who goes? Most people use job skills, experience, efficiency, and ability to work hard as their criteria.

Let's see. Jerry is a hard worker who's been here forever and is the only person who really knows the process from start to finish. He stays, right? Wrong! Jerry may stay, but not for those reasons. The person making the decision does not work closely with Jerry and has no idea how good he is.

You can also forget your hope that somebody will get rid of Wilson, who in a year has learned nothing except how to goof off and ignore people who know what they're talking about. The person deciding about your job won't know what a good worker you are, or what a lazy guy Wilson is. That person will have a list of salaries and a financial goal.

People like Jerry, with years of experience, are often paid at the top of their scales. Newer employees like Bill are usually paid less. To the people upstairs, the two do the same work but one costs less. It's an easy call.

Downsizing decisions are seldom based on how well you work or even on how much the company needs your skills. This is where the paranoia comes in. What if you're an employee with great experience, skill, and a higher price tag (of which you're worth every penny)? How do you protect yourself from the false security of the Sacred Bull who whispers, "Trust me. You're safe. People should know how good you are"?

You can increase your odds by looking at yourself and your department through the decision maker's eyes and doing what you can to make your position stronger. Downsizing is a financial decision. The most effective defense against it is to be square in the middle of the department with the best bottom line.

If you don't want to transfer, you need to do some PR work now. Don't assume that people will know about your value to the company. If you want to save your job, you have to be able to demonstrate its monetary value. How much money do you save the company? How much money does your work bring in? How does your work lead to repeat business or bigger orders? What makes you worth more than you cost?

If you have a clear idea of how your company really views the question of who stays and who goes, you can better influence in which column your name lands.

A SYSTEMS ANALYST BITES THE DUST

Most managers reward and promote people who learn by observation and figure out the system. Managers see them as highly motivated winners. Those who cannot recognize what system they're in face problems. Consider Alex, whose story of burnout is repeated in thousands of companies every day.

Alex, a systems analyst for a large, high-tech firm, is feeling heavy frustration at work. Two months ago he went through a long application process for a promotion to project manager, but he didn't get it. He probably could have handled that setback all right if the job had gone to somebody qualified. But the promotion went to Drew, and all the guys in the department know that Drew's grasp of the job's technical aspects are pretty slippery.

In fact, Alex thinks Drew is all-around slippery. He's not exactly a liar, but Drew seems to tell people, especially management, what they want to hear. When management proposes changes in procedure or suggests things the department can do to improve, Drew is always the guy saying, "No problem."

Sure, it's no problem to him. Alex and the rest of the guys are the ones who'll be doing the work. Most of the time Alex is sure Drew doesn't even understand what's involved. Instead of spending time in Systems, Drew is always getting himself appointed to committees with all the PR types from upstairs, or off doing lunch with somebody, or in some pointless meeting. Anything to get out of doing honest work. Alex still can't believe it. Why would they promote a guy like Drew, who is nothing but a lazy, incompetent, political sleaze?

Yesterday was the last straw for Alex. Another project manager position had come open, and Alex figured his turn had finally come. He went to tell Anne, the VP of operations, that he was putting his hat in the ring. He expected her to give him a thumbs-up and say, "It's yours for the asking. You've earned it."

But Anne told him she couldn't back him; he had "an attitude problem and lacked sufficient 'people skills.'"

Alex felt himself burning out, right there in Anne's office.

He went home last night and figured out how soon he could apply for early retirement. Until then, he'll keep his head down, give them his eight hours, and get the heck out the door every night.

Alex, the systems analyst, lost out because he did not try to analyze the system he was part of. When Drew was promoted, Alex missed a key lesson. He did not recognize that the company prized and rewarded political behavior like Drew's, which they could see, more than Alex's hard work and competence, which they couldn't. Alex saw Drew's promotion as an indication of the incompetence of top management rather than a statement of their clear preference.

Alex was talented, knowledgeable, and highly skilled. His dissatisfaction and burnout would become a big loss to the company, one that its managers could have prevented. Their first mistake was promoting someone who looked good to them but did not have the respect of his peers. They could have checked out how Drew was viewed before deciding whom to promote.

A manager needed to tell Alex and others like him what the company really valued and what he would have to do to get a promotion. Everything Alex heard led him to believe that his hard work and competence would be rewarded. His skills were eventually wasted because the company assumed that, if Alex were project manager material, he would have known how to get ahead without being told.

WHEN THE COMPANY EXPECTS MIND READING

Some of the things you need to know we can tell you. A lot of the things you are not told have to do with the image and attitude you project rather than the specifics of how you do your job. To be effective in any job, you have to know how to make a good impression. What can you do to anticipate your boss's expectations and project yourself as a highly motivated, efficient, and savvy employee?

What You See Is Not Necessarily What You Get

In many companies, "looking good"—understanding the system without being told—is rewarded more than actually doing the job well. This is because it is much easier and more immediate to see who looks good, rather than to regularly check to see who is doing a good job. For most managers, doing a good job is very hard to measure; looking good is easy to see.

This helps to explain the overwhelming importance of appearance and positive attitude in most companies. People who look good and act upbeat and positive are seen as being smarter, more creative, and nicer than people who dress differently, have an unusual hairstyle, or grumble and complain. Of course, these external qualities may have nothing to do with how well people perform their jobs. In most cases, however, they do determine how people are judged. People just "know" who the winners are.

To be considered a winner, you have to be able to pick up corporate culture by mind reading. Like internal competition, it is another fact of life in most companies that drives people crazy. The more you talk about it and explain it, however, the less complicated and intimidating it may be.

Mind Reading Survival Skills

The following suggestions will help you give the impression that you know what to do without being told. You probably know some of these already. Think about how you learned them. Did you have to figure them out for yourself? Were you told informally by a veteran employee? In most workplaces, these things are not spelled out explicitly. Even if you think they are obvious, consider all the people who don't—your employees, for instance.

Come in.   Even if the manual says it's there, regularly using all of your sick leave marks you as an outsider. Of course, everyone is ill once in awhile, but regularly missing a day or two here and there (especially on Mondays and Fridays) will brand you as someone who doesn't have a clue about what it takes to get ahead in your company.

Identify with your company.   Act, speak, and behave as if what's good for the company is good for you. Think twice before complaining. If you act as if your boss is your adversary, you're asking for trouble (as well as displaying that your own problems with authority are more important to you than doing a good job).

Watch your boss.   Observe how your boss dresses, acts in meetings, practices small talk, and uses his or her time. Most important, learn your boss's priorities and follow them. Never mind if they seem wrong to you. Succeeding at your job often depends on seeing it from your boss's point of view rather than from your own.

Have a professional appearance.   Every company has its own standards for dress, and it's best to conform to them. A rule of thumb for dressing for work is not to wear anything that will call attention to you. (We know it's your right to wear anything you want, but it's also your right to wave a red flag in front of a Sacred Bull, and you know where that can land you.)

Be pleasant.   Make a real effort to get along with the people you work with. If you're upset about someone, try to deal calmly, courteously, and directly with the person.

Don't take your problems to everyone who wanders into your office. Eliminate snorting, eye rolling, and a conspicuous frown. Do your best to avoid participating in squabbles with coworkers. A squabble will tarnish your image.

Take direction and criticism.   It would be great if your boss were more specific and more positive; but in work, as in poker, you need to play the hand you're dealt.

Do your job as if it were worth doing.   Know enough about your job to know all that it involves. Don't make your boss have to remind you. Give your best effort to all the parts of your job, including the parts that nobody regularly checks.

Offer criticism and suggestions constructively.   Don't tell your boss everything he or she is doing wrong. Pick your battles well. Make an occasional suggestion about how something could be done better, but realize that, in business, everything has a price tag. Even if your idea is great, know without being told that its ultimate cost usually will determine whether it will be accepted.

Have a sense of humor.   Especially about yourself. No one likes to work with people who take themselves too seriously. Pay particular attention to keeping a sense of humor about your politics, your illnesses and allergies, your pets, and your children.

These are basic social and political skills that are required for virtually any job if you want to present an acceptable image. They are the kinds of things you are supposed to pick up by mind reading at most workplaces. You're expected to have learned them before you started working. In kindergarten? At home? Yet these skills are specific to work settings; they are not what you do in school or at home.

They are also not that hard to talk about. Although extremely difficult to turn into written rules, these are the basic unwritten rules in most companies. There are times when all of these rules can and should be broken. To get the specifics for your company, you will have to ask around and watch people who are successful. Think carefully about exactly what they are doing and do it yourself as best you can.

BANISHING THE BULL OF MIND READING

The real test of your skill as a manager is the effect you have on the bottom 80 percent of people, the ones who don't know how to manage you and need you to manage them. These people *are* paying attention to some cues about what they should do and how they should behave. The problem is that they may not be paying attention to the cues that you want them to pick up.

The way to manage the people who need help figuring out what it takes to make a good impression and do their jobs well requires you to banish the Bull of Mind Reading. The more you rely on real managing and the less on mind reading, the more effective you will be. To be most effective in teaching employees what you want, you have to provide as much information as possible.

The following strategies will help you overcome the tendency to assume employees should "just know" what you want from them.

Know what you want. The Bull of Mind Reading is not very proactive. It is more likely to think, "They should have known better" than to think clearly about the complex skills and fine discrimination people need to know. Before you teach, understand exactly what you want people to learn. Let people know in advance what they're supposed to do, when it's due, and how they can please you.

Ask for what you want and reward it when you get it. Don't assume that people know what to do. Like everyone else, managers need to ask for what they want. Most people know the basics of the job. What you need to ask for specifically are matters of style—*how* people do things—and sensitivity to the political realities of your company.

Assume that all the people you manage know about these areas is what you tell them. Set priorities and let people know what is most important, even if you think they should already know. Explain complex skills by breaking them down into a series of manageable tasks. Use examples that apply to your team. Set priorities for each step. Encourage questions as you teach.

Reward good work. Any behavior followed by a reward will happen more often. This basic rule of human behavior seems most difficult for managers who follow the Sacred Bull of Mind Reading. Praise is a superfluous technique if you believe people should already know what they're supposed to do.

The typical strategy of managers who believe in mind reading is, "As long as employees are doing what they're supposed to be doing, ignore them. When they step out of line, punish them." As we will see in chapter 6 on blame, punishing negative behavior is much less effective than rewarding positive behavior. The more payoff there is for doing what you want, the more likely you are to get it.

Ask for behaviors, not attitudes. Don't try to instill an attitude and assume that it will lead to correct behaviors. The more practical your material, the better. Show people what you want them to do and tell them why they should do it. Don't worry about what they're thinking while they're doing it.

If you just tell people the attitudes they should have, you are asking for mind reading. Concepts such as motivation, initiative, and entrepreneurship have very different meanings to different people. Rather than making a list of attributes and expecting people to figure out what the list means, your best strategy is to teach people how to *show* that they have all the positive attributes the company values.

Talk to your employees. Ask about and listen to their concerns. Ask questions to determine how sophisticated their understanding is of how things really are. The better you know them, the better you'll know what they need to know. Short, regular meetings for this purpose are helpful. (When you've scheduled one of these sessions, don't cancel.) The more you can get your employees to talk to you, the more effective you can be as their boss. After all, what do they expect you to be—a mind reader?

Tell it like it is, even if it's embarrassing. You have to be explicit about what you want people to do in certain situations. Give them examples of what is appropriate or inappropriate, even if the examples are difficult or embarrassing for you. Believe us, you will be much more embarrassed if people you manage don't know these things.

SHOULD PEOPLE GIVE YOU WHAT YOU WANT?

We have been assuming so far that if you're a manager, you should be clear and specific about what you want so that people will know how to please you. This is certainly good advice. It beats expecting people to know what to do without being told. But what if pleasing you is not necessarily the best way to do things?

GARY'S RULES

Gary has always lived by a set of internal rules, the things his father taught him by example about how a man should live:

- *A job worth doing is worth doing well.*
- *Push yourself to your limits.*

- *Work hard; don't complain.*
- *Work before you play.*
- *Most of all, put the job first.*

All of Gary's internal rules have to do with work. To him, how you work is the measure of a man. It's not that he's a workaholic. He spends time with his family and has hobbies, but when he's at work, he feels strong obligations to behave according to the decorum that he was taught. Work is what a man does, and he does it with dignity.

Gary takes his duties very seriously. He keeps his group as organized as he does his desk. His subordinates trust him to be firm but fair—and totally by the book. Gary's style is straightforward, predictable, and steady, if conventional and a bit distant and chilly.

Mario, on the other hand, is expansive, emotional to the point of being in-your-face erratic, and creative. He's always griping, he doesn't take care of details, and he just doesn't take things seriously enough. On most tasks that he's not interested in, he does the bare minimum needed to get by. (One of Gary's Rules is that the work dictates what needs to be done, not your own personal likes and dislikes.) If Mario is working on something he likes, however, the word genius *is not misapplied.*

Mario supplies the department with a lot of qualities that Gary lacks (for starters, creativity, levity, and fun). He's definitely the idea person. He's also the departmental cutup (and, at times, the departmental screwup). Mario also is brilliant. His ideas have been the impetus for many of the department's most successful projects. Of course, his brainstorms would have come to nothing without the hard work that Gary and the rest put into them.

Gary knows, at least in his head, that Mario is important to the department. But he just can't bring himself to approve of him, much less like him. Mario's style is so informal and irreverent; everything he does seems to irritate

Gary. Like the time Mario turned the company logo into a lewd cartoon, made copies, and passed them around at the staff meeting. He should know better than that! Or the clothes he wears: fluorescent ties with pictures of Bugs Bunny and Porky Pig. Or the incessant singing in his office: old Rolling Stones lyrics mostly. The guy never stops acting like a teenager.

Gary's promotion has come through and he's department head—and Mario's boss. For years Gary had been saying to himself, "If I were in charge of this department, I wouldn't let him get away with this kind of stuff." In the past he dealt with Mario by shaking his head and avoiding him. Now Gary is responsible for him.

Many of the things Gary knew without being told, Mario has never heard of or doesn't care about. At first Gary thought of transferring him, but he realized that would be taking the easy way out—not allowed under Gary's Rules.

Gary met with Mario several times. The meetings were uneasy and very formal. Gary wanted to lay down some rules but realized how petty and irrelevant it would sound to say, "No Porky Pig and 'Honky Tonk Woman' on company time." Instead, Gary said a few things about decorum and let it go at that.

Mario left the final "decorum" meeting wondering if he had a future in the department.

Later a few people in the department stopped by Gary's office. They all seemed to make positive comments about Mario. Gary may be a little stiff, but he wasn't stupid. Everybody was worried that he was going to transfer Mario or drive him out by clamping down on him so tightly that he would have to go.

It was a shock to Gary that people had read his mind so accurately. He didn't like what they saw. Gary has rules against abusing power, and he saw that he was heading in that direction. He could not allow himself to abuse his power by getting rid of a valuable team member because of *his own prejudice. (It was hard for him to admit, but Mario is valuable. Even harder to admit was his own prejudice against Mario's personal style.)*

Gary also began to see that his rules were good for him, *but they weren't universal. A department full of Garys would be easy to manage but would not do the job nearly as well as one with different personalities and skills.*

Gary consulted his rules and discovered that his own values were not consistent with imposing those values on everyone. The choice was clear. Gary's chief obligation was to the department, and the department wanted Mario. Gary would have to develop a working relationship with him.

Until now, Gary's internal rules have been the "givens" of his existence at work. They have helped him do a good job. For the first time, however, he sees that they're getting in the way. For all the careful and hard work he did, Gary discovered that he inhibited creativity and, often, discussion. Mario was the only one in the department willing to risk his disapproval. Everybody else knew, without being told, to tone it down when Gary was around.

The more Gary thought about it (and talked about it with his wife, his most trusted adviser), the more he began to see that his style was, in its own way, as extreme as Mario's—better for some things, but not for all.

Gary began to see his irritation at Mario as his problem and not Mario's. He met with Mario again. This time he was clearer about what he had to say.

"Mario, it's no secret that our styles are different. It's also no secret that this department needs you, and needs you pretty much the way you are. I expect that you and I are going to be working together for a long time. We need to be able to get along.

"We need to tolerate each other, and when we don't, we

need to handle it privately and face to face. I will be open to what you have to say about me, and I expect the same courtesy. Do we have a deal?"

Because of Mario, Gary's Rules expanded to include tolerance. He realized that management meant more than expecting everyone to do things his way.

Gary has a responsibility to manage the department. It would be easy to get everyone to adapt to his style and give him what he wanted without his even having to ask. Gary has seen plenty of managers do it that way. But that just doesn't fit with Gary's internal rules. The job comes first—before the comfort of the manager. His father would be proud.

A few years later, Gary was promoted to CEO. His first choice for executive VP was Mario. You can see their picture in the company newsletter: Mario in a dignified gray suit, and Gary decorous as always. But if you look very closely, the little dots on Gary's proper maroon tie are really tiny faces of Porky Pig.

Chapter Six

THE BULL OF BLAME
It Has to Be Somebody's Fault

The Wilson job didn't come through. Larry heard the news at the morning meeting, and he still can't believe it. Back in his office, he stares into his coffee and fumes to himself.

. . . I can't believe Elise blew it like this. She thinks she's Ms. Sophistication with her la-di-da Marketing Department. She should have been selling the contract, but all she did was take a few Wilson managers out to lunch, where she could demonstrate her so-called savoir faire. I'll bet it really impressed them how well she could order wine. Yeah, right.

. . . Did she even once call me in—or anybody else from Engineering—to show the Wilson team that we have the know-how to do the job? No way. She was probably afraid we'd slurp coffee from our saucers or something.

. . . No, instead Little Ms. Marketing wrote us off. "It's a sensitive negotiation, Larry. We have to be delicate, Larry, get to know them, establish rapport." Rapport, my hind end. What a bunch of bull.

Larry already knows a few of the guys at Wilson, by reputation anyway. They're engineering types.

... We could have gotten the contract if we'd shown 'em some nuts-and-bolts stuff. Instead Elise is running up outrageous restaurant tabs and filling the Wilson people full of quiche and white wine.

Larry knows he could have made more headway taking them out for a beer and showing them a few sketches. How could Elise have been so stupid?

When something goes wrong, nothing is more human than to try to find out who is to blame. Few responses, however, are more damaging to your long-term psychological health. Take Larry, for example. He already has created some big problems for himself, and he's about to make them bigger. The Wilson job was very important to his company and his department. The loss is a major problem and a complex one. In his mind, Larry is turning the whole issue into a matter more simple, easier to understand—and incorrect: It's all Elise's fault.

There is something primitive and satisfying about the process. It would not take much to convince Larry that throwing Elise into a live volcano as an offering to the Contract Gods would make the situation better.

Let's look at the situation more objectively, however, and see what Larry is really doing. At the simplest level, he is making himself angry. He is taking a spark of irritation and fanning it into a flame of rage. The more he runs the story over in his mind, the angrier he becomes. As his anger goes up, his ability to think decreases. (One formula they didn't teach in Engineering School is that intelligence is inversely proportional to emotional arousal. The angrier you get, the more IQ points you lose.)

As Larry's ability to think melts away in the furnace of his anger, the more he believes that the way to fix the situation is to do something about Elise.

THE BULL OF BLAME CAN CLOUD YOUR MIND

The Bull of Blame has the power to cloud men's minds (women's, too). He can convince you that all you have to do to fix a problem is to figure out whose fault it is and punish that person. Never mind that punishment does nothing to make the situation better. It feels so right, as if you're really doing something productive.

The angrier you become, the easier it is to justify destructive action, and the more attractive the idea of punishment seems. You can even invent reasons why acting out subcortical impulses makes perfectly good sense. The Bull of Blame can turn a rational, reasonable person into a snarling, drooling beast—and a self-righteous one, at that. And this is just what happens internally. The Bull can also lead you to do some very self-destructive things on the outside.

Larry has finished his coffee and gets up to get another cup. He stalks down the hall, fuming and muttering things that sound like "savoir faire" and "quiche." The first person who asks, "What's up, Larry?" will get the complete story of Elise's incompetence as Larry has been creating it inside his head, in technicolor and cinemascope, with close-ups of the white wine and quiche.

By lunchtime the story will be all over the building.

Elise has already heard it three times, each version more embellished than the last. "Do you know what Larry is saying about you?"

Yes, I know, Elise thinks, staring into her already cool cup of Darjeeling. What a horse's rear end that guy is. Subtle as a Sherman tank but not quite as bright. The real reason the Wilson job fell through is because his department isn't flexible and creative enough to give Wilson anything like what they want. They knew about other jobs we did and were skeptical about our ability to come through with what they needed.

. . . All the while, Larry kept pushing me to let him "have a crack at them." He actually used those words. That would really have been a help. Larry would have been happy to come over and lecture them on how engineering must be done—circa 1968, the last time he had a new idea. The Wilson team would never have spoken to us again.

. . . Obviously, the real problem is Larry. Until the Engineering Department gets some new leadership, we're going to blow more and more of these contracts. I can't believe that idiot is saying I lost this one. The guy is barely qualified to be a mechanic, much less head an engineering department.

Elise takes a sip of cold tea, frowns, and walks down the hall to brew another cup. On the way she runs into Miguel, who asks, "What's up, Elise?"

By lunchtime the next day the whole company has chosen sides. Some think the problem would be best solved by firing Elise. Others think it's Larry who should get the axe. Lost somewhere in the dust of combat is the Wilson job— why it was lost and what its loss can teach the entire company. But nobody has time for that. A fight is so much more interesting.

When people start blaming someone else and prepare to defend against an attack, the accompanying burst of adrenaline knocks out some of their more advanced mental functions. (Amazing the way the loss of a few IQ points can bring complex problems down to a manageable level.) The most complicated situation can instantly turn into a simple, finger-pointing, personal conflict: *Larry* v. *Elise*.

Most disturbing, when people are functioning at this diminished capacity, their judgment is so impaired that they think they're doing something constructive. If we agree with them, we are making the same mistake in judgment.

Alexander Pope said, "Blame is safer than praise." It is also much easier. If you praise something, people can always tell you what's wrong with it. When something is wrong, it is easier to point the finger than to try to fix the problem. Finger pointing can turn any complex issue into a fight.

FIXING THE BLAME DOES NOT FIX THE PROBLEM

In business very few problems are truly personal. Most problems are caused by the way the entire system, consisting of many people and departments, deals with certain issues. *Systemic* problems are the result of the way things are structured and the pressure that system places on people to act in certain ways.

People do what is rewarded, and they try to avoid punishment as best they can. Sometimes the structure of a company or department can create unintended contingencies that push people toward actions that may not be best for the company as a whole.

Jon works for an insurance company in Eligibility and Claims. People work on claims together, of course, but basically one person does a part, then sends the file on to the next person to do another part.

Jon's department manager demands efficiency, which means a quick turnaround. Difficult claims take too much time. Jon knows if you take too much time on one case, your in-basket starts stacking up and your output starts going down. Then the trouble begins. Jon has discovered that he can work up a claim and cover over some of the problems: Just don't mention a few little pieces of information and pass the file along to someone else.

He sees cases like this as ticking bombs. The object of the game is to get the bomb off his desk as quickly as possible and hope it explodes in another department. Eventually, somebody will be stuck with it, but that's not Jon's problem. Let the bomb mess up somebody else's stats.

A typical response to this situation is to see Jon as a poor employee who deserves discipline. Catch him sending out a few of his little bombs and punish him. (End of problem.) That is what the Bull of Blame wants you to think. Maybe Jon should be more conscientious, but that is actually a minor point compared with the situation that induces him to act as he does.

The fact that people are judged by output alone puts a premium on getting a claim off your desk and onto someone else's as quickly as possible. There is no reward for being conscientious. People like Jon recognize the incentives in the situation, so they do things that hamper the efficiency of the whole department.

Unfortunately it is much easier to think in terms of personal malfeasance than in terms of a systemic problem. However, blaming individuals for messing up will only compound a systemic problem.

THE REIGN OF TERRIBLE TANYA

The poor efficiency of the Claims Department is legendary throughout the company. Finally management decides it's time for some new blood, someone who will really crack down and make sure people are doing what they're supposed to do. They hire Tanya.

Tanya actually goes around with a ruler and measures the size of the stack of claims on people's desks. If the stack is more than twelve inches high, she considers people bottlenecks. She chews them out soundly and rates their efficiency lower on their evaluations.

Performance does improve. Turnaround does speed up. Management thinks Terrible Tanya is just what they need.

If they had more managers like her, things would really shape up. They think about sending her to Customer Service, where the time it takes to handle complaints is going way up. What they need is some efficiency down there, like the kind Tanya brought to Eligibility and Claims.

The real "efficiency" wasn't discovered until years later, when the office was remodeled. Workers were astounded to discover hundreds of claim forms tucked above the acoustic tiles in the suspended ceiling over Tanya's department.

When members of her team got difficult cases that would cause the stacks of files on their desk to build up, they just filed them away above the ceiling, rather than risk blame and punishment for being bottlenecks.

The real problem at the insurance company was not Tanya's punitive style or Jon's shiftlessness. It was the fact that everyone was rewarded or punished based on how fast they turned work around. The incentives were to toss the problems to someone else or hide them in the ceiling. The irony is that the most conscientious workers were the ones who ended up being seen as bottlenecks.

Our tendency to blame tells us that fixing the blame is as good as fixing the problem. When something goes wrong, all we have to do is find the people who messed up and punish them. This strategy is emotionally satisfying and it seems so right. Never mind that it usually makes the situation worse.

The Sacred Bull of Blame is strong enough that if people have the power to use punishment, they may abuse it unless there is some way to prevent it. One solution is a grievance system that really works. Even better is paying regular attention to how people feel about their jobs and whether they believe they are being singled out for punishment. An open discussion of what is appropriate and inappropriate use of punishment by a manager might also be helpful.

THE VICTIM TRAP

The idea that someone must be to blame can make people do a lot of ill-considered things. It can lead them to simplify complex problems. It can divert people from the actual problem to something that is simpler and more satisfying to deal with. It can lead managers to rely on punishment, which is easy to use but makes the problem worse. It can create the fear and distrust that is so damaging in a business, as we explained in chapter 4.

Using blame in these ways is destructive enough, but wait until you see what the Bull of Blame can do to you on the inside.

This Bull will pick you up when you're down. Maybe that's why this dangerous creature is so often mistaken for a friend—your only friend.

"Who did this to you?" he asks. "It has to be somebody's fault!

"It's a well-known fact," he snorts, already beginning to paw the ground. "You can't feel better until you know. You and I will find out together!"

Let's look at how blame works individually. Blame offers a quick fix when something goes wrong. The natural tendency when something goes wrong is to feel hurt or sad. These feelings are difficult to bear. It feels better to be angry—and most of us are willing to trade our feelings of hurt and sadness for anger at the earliest chance.

Anger is easier to bear than sadness. When you're sad, you just want to sit and be sad. When you're angry, you're more activated. You want to get up and do something, such as finding the guy who got you into this fix and letting him have it. Never mind that an eruption does nothing to solve your problem and often makes it worse. Many powerful people react this way, and maybe if you get mad enough, you'll get some power, too.

Also, getting angry is doing something. Everybody knows that it's better to do something than to sit around feeling sorry for yourself. Right?

The logic of that last statement, like most Sacred Bull, is convincing, compelling, and utterly wrong. Of course, we are not saying that sitting around feeling sorry for yourself is a good thing. What we dispute is that getting angry and finding someone to blame is different from feeling sorry for yourself. Take it from someone who has made a living listening to people talk about their problems. Getting angry is not the opposite of feeling sorry for yourself. It is a necessary prerequisite.

Blaming is just a louder, more active form of feeling sorry for yourself. It may start with shouting and pointing the finger of righteous indignation outward. But it ends in a silent feeling of helplessness. Then the finger turns and points inward, and you inevitably start to blame yourself. You may bounce back and forth between anger and self-pity, feeling more helpless each time. You have paid very dearly for a temporary jolt of adrenaline. The price is the feeling of control over what happens to you.

LUCAS FALLS INTO THE VICTIM TRAP

Lucas could almost taste the bitterness when, at the staff meeting, the board chairman announced the company would do an outside search to replace Meredith, the outgoing executive director. Everybody knew Lucas expected to get the job. He had made that clear in words and actions since Meredith announced she would retire at the end of the year.

Amanda had announced an interest in the job, too, but she just couldn't be serious. Lucas had been with the agency eleven years, eight in management positions. Amanda had been there barely two. She had hit the ground running, with all kinds of wild ideas that cost a lot of money and seemed directed mostly at her own self-promotion.

Lucas had pegged her from the start as self-serving, out for her own personal gain instead of thinking of the good of the agency, as he did. She was sneaky, conniving, and a rumormonger. Lucas was always having to set people straight about the rumors she passed about him.

Amanda had been stirring up trouble since the day she arrived. In the months since Meredith announced her upcoming retirement, things had gotten worse. How could that troublemaker think she had what it takes to be executive director? She must know there was no chance that she would be considered a serious candidate, yet here she was, trying to keep him from getting the job.

In the past few months Lucas believed he had made it clear at every opportunity that Amanda lacked experience and the kind of fiscal good sense the agency needed. Meanwhile, she had planted her share of "suggestions" about him, such as saying he was too entrenched in the factional politics and that he had too much history with the agency. Talk about the pot calling the kettle black! There hadn't been any factional politics until Amanda arrived.

Lucas had been sure that nobody saw her as a serious candidate. He had a strong base of support throughout the agency, and she had two or three people—troublemakers like herself. The one person he couldn't read was Meredith. One day she sent signals that he was her choice; the next, she seemed all buddy-buddy with Amanda.

When Lucas heard the chairman's announcement, he realized that Amanda had gotten to enough people to seriously harm his chances. The board chairman and Meredith herself were saying that the agency needed to take a different direction. The past has been marred by too much "factional politics," they said, and the agency needed someone who could bring everybody together. Lucas knew where they had gotten that rhetoric.

At least Amanda wouldn't get the job, but Lucas knew that she and her behind-the-scenes dealing had ruined his chances. From now on, he would know who the enemy was.

Lucas was ignoring something that was painfully obvious to everyone else at the agency. His politicking for the director's position and his smear campaign against Amanda had increased the factionalism. People saw him as politicking himself right out of the job.

Meredith, the retiring director, had done little to help the situation. Her attempts at being evenhanded involved supporting first Lucas, then Amanda. Most people were hoping for a new director who could help everyone move beyond the in-house conflict.

Amanda had been politicking, too, but Lucas was correct about her chances. Nobody really saw her as a serious candidate. Most people agreed that Lucas would have done better to ignore her rather than stir things up at every opportunity.

The result for Lucas was a headfirst fall into the Victim Trap. Instead of acknowledging to himself that he was hurt and sad about losing the job, he was bubbling with resentment. He believed Amanda had blocked his career.

GETTING STUCK ON ANGER AND BLAME

When people face disappointment or loss at work, they go through stages similar to the stages involved in accepting profound change of any kind. The stages usually begin with shock and disbelief, followed by anger and sadness. The usual pattern is to bounce back and forth between anger and sadness for awhile. This is followed by a period of problem solving and, finally, acceptance.

We wish we could say that these stages follow a set and orderly pattern, that they last a specific amount of time and then are over. Instead, the stages vary from person to person. People often move back and forth between stages as they go through the process of mourning, acceptance, and moving on.

It is easy to get stuck on anger and blame. Anger is far more acceptable in business settings than sadness. Anger is activating. People can use it as a motivation to keep going. Although anger can get a person to do things, however, they are seldom the right things. Anger just keeps bubbling along, with hurt below the surface to fuel it. The way out of the Victim Trap is through sadness.

You get stuck in the Victim Trap when you begin to accept the anger stage as more real than the sadness or the other emotions that loss generates. Most of us feel anger for a short while, of course, but can move on to other stages. The unfortunate few get themselves trapped in the feeling that someone has done this to them. The only solution they see is that something (usually some form of punishment) needs to happen to set things right. Only then, they believe, can they move on.

Until they get out of this basic pattern of thinking, they will not be going anywhere but down.

THE VIEW FROM THE VICTIM TRAP

There is very little psychological difference between blaming someone else and blaming yourself. The idea of blame and punishment causes the endless loop that keeps people in the Victim Trap. You punish; you don't feel better; you look around for someone or something else that is making you feel so bad. You blame that, and the cycle continues. It doesn't matter whether you are blaming others or yourself. As long as you are blaming and trying to punish, there is no way out.

All the while, your perception becomes distorted. You move into the victim position, where you merely react to whatever is done to you. Someone or something else has taken control of all the important actions in your life. Often these actions are in the past, out of reach and impossible to change. It is easy then to become demoralized and to feel hopeless and helpless. Your only reality is something that has already happened that you cannot fix.

Within the Victim Trap, all you can do at this point is try to punish the person you blame or to get other people to realize the terrible thing that has happened to you. Sad people are sad; it is the angry people who feel sorry for themselves.

Lucas's bitterness is still bubbling three years later. By now he is bitter not only toward Amanda and the new director, Roosevelt, but toward nearly everyone and everything else at the agency.

Nothing suits Lucas. Everything is wrong here. He has grave doubts about whether the agency is really performing its mission or whether it will even survive much longer.

Everyone else is hopeful. Roosevelt is a good manager and has made some positive changes. The only real problem left is Lucas. He's still influential as a kind of "leader of the opposition" to whatever there is to oppose at the moment. He calls it being a devil's advocate and sees it as a positive function. Everybody else thinks he never misses a chance to shoot things down.

None of this makes Lucas feel better. Inside, he just can't forgive the agency for not choosing him as director. He may get a few programs derailed and win a battle or two occasionally, but Lucas lost the war a long time ago.

His work is suffering. Some people joke about it as on-site early retirement. Roosevelt has had to take him aside and counsel him more than once. But Lucas feels that "Rosey" is just prejudiced against him because of Amanda, who has obviously prospered under the new regime.

Amanda was upset and angry, too, about not getting the

director's position. She had known she was a long shot but thought she could turn herself into a real possibility by playing her cards right. When Roosevelt was hired, she realized that she had badly overplayed her hand. She had created a credibility problem for herself by engaging in factional politics.

She was still angry at Lucas, but she came to the sober conclusion that she would have to let her anger go and change her ways to be seen as more of a team player. If not, she might as well leave the agency right then because her career would be over.

Amanda got behind Rosey and his new programs. She even made a special point of saying positive things about Lucas, not that it made much difference in how he felt about her. Her feelings about him began to change, however. Instead of seeing him as devious, she saw him more and more as someone stuck in a situation he couldn't control. She wished she could help him, but she knew Lucas would never accept anything from her except a fight.

By letting go of her anger, Amanda was able to get beyond becoming Lucas's victim. She realized that she could have some control over her situation if she changed the way she acted. She was still sad and hurt about not getting what she wanted, but she was able to look to the future rather than staying stuck in the past.

This was not easy. She had to face some unpleasant truths about herself and do something about them. What Amanda gained for her trouble was a feeling of control over her life. The feeling went far deeper than the "Believe in yourself and you'll get everything you want" spouted at motivational seminars. She had to take responsibility for what she had done to herself and make some decisions about what she was going to do to change. The experience gave her some positive insights.

Believing You Are in Control

You are in control of what you do, but you may have less control over what you get for it. You may not control what you get, but you may control how you feel about it.

This may sound like a semantic game, but it is the single issue most related to psychological health. A perception of control over what happens to you, not complete control itself, is what is important.

You don't control the cards you're dealt, but you do control how you play your hand. People who have this perception fare far better than those who don't. They are more successful materially, they are less susceptible to stress, and they even live longer. They look less at what went wrong and more at what they can do about it.

Often it takes real adversity for you to develop this perception. The reason we don't all feel this way is that, in the short run, it is much easier to rely on the Bull of Blame. Psychologically, however, the worst thing you can do is see yourself as a victim.

In most cases, if you see yourself as a victim, you give up your ability to act, to choose, or to heal yourself. Instead, all you can do is point the finger of blame and tell the world what was done to you and why that exempts you from responsibility for whatever else happens. This is not a satisfying life; it is hardly a life at all. It is, however, a strong temptation when bad things happen.

It is easy to fall into the Victim Trap, to believe that, because you have no control over what happens to you, you have no control over your reaction to it. You may even feel some perverse satisfaction in believing that your diminished life is someone else's doing. So what if the price of that satisfaction is your future? At least it doesn't feel like your fault.

To stay psychologically healthy, you have to be able to mourn your losses and move on. To feel successful inside—to avoid feeling sorry for yourself—you have to avoid the temptation to blame and, instead, to recognize your own control.

Back at the agency five years later, Roosevelt has been unexpectedly called to his reward. (No, he didn't die. Administrations changed and he was given a prestigious federal appointment.) The board hardly had to search this time. Amanda is the new executive director.

For Lucas, this is the final trick of cruel fate. "Just you wait," he says to his cronies. "Her first act is going to be to get rid of me. She can't have any rivals around." He knows he's going to be victimized again. He can't do anything about it, but he feels a certain martyr's purity about accepting it.

Amanda is also thinking that she will have to let Lucas go. Not because he's a rival; he ceased being that long ago. Lucas is not doing his job, and he's insubordinate, too. He's asking for it, and Amanda knows it's only a matter of time before she has to give it to him. What a waste. She remembers the days when Lucas was knowledgeable, competent, and a real leader. But that was before he got caught in the Victim Trap.

THE TERRIBLE MEEK

The Victim Trap has teeth. One of the worst things about blame and punishment is that they tend to get passed along to innocent bystanders. People who have been hurt tend to think of hurting back.

People who have been punished, discriminated against, or otherwise victimized feel angry. Seldom, however, can they take out their anger on whoever really hurt them. Some will settle for targets of opportunity. Often the people closest to them—family members, coworkers, and subordinates—are the ones who get the passed-on punishment.

This is usually not a conscious choice. People who see themselves as victims have a great deal of free-floating anger. When they see something they don't like, pow, out it comes. They don't mean to erupt, but it happens nevertheless. After the explosion, they can usually justify their behavior.

Victims tend to patrol their boundaries carefully to make sure no one is making unauthorized forays into their territory or taking advantage of them. To them, small incursions are just as invasive as big ones. The Bull of Blame teaches his victims an indelible lesson: Once you've been burned, you have to stand up for yourself; you have to watch out. Don't let anybody forget you're a victim.

"What's the matter with Dad? Why is he always yelling at us?" Lucas's nine-year-old daughter, near tears, whispered to her mother after Lucas had thrown down his napkin and stormed from the table again, leaving his dinner half-eaten. "I didn't mean to spill my milk in his salad, and I said I was sorry. He used to make jokes and stuff when he came home. Now he's mad at us all the time. What are we doing that's so bad?"

Before his wife could answer, Lucas reappeared in the kitchen doorway. Hanging his head and sighing loudly, he said, "You're not doing anything wrong, honey. Daddy is really sorry. I'm just under a lot of bad pressure at work. People there . . . well, they're kind of being mean to your old dad, and I guess I just haven't been my old self lately."

Lucas's wife gave him a look of mixed annoyance and sympathy. He was out of line for yelling at the kids and throwing a tantrum. He'd been so short fused lately. The milk in the lettuce was just the latest in a series of little incidents that set him off. In fact, he'd been crying over spilled milk ever since that witch Amanda had gotten the job that Lucas deserved. Every night he came home with another horror story about the ways Amanda and her faction had turned the agency against him.

His wife didn't know whether to hug him or yell at him. "Do you want me to warm up your dinner?" she asked.

"No, thanks, honey." Lucas sank back into his chair. "I'll just eat it cold."

She sighed (all this sighing must be contagious, she thought) and gave the kids permission to leave the table. When she and Lucas were alone in the kitchen, she watched him for a moment as he picked listlessly at his ruined meal. Suddenly a flash of irritation swept through her. Lucas's wife leaned toward him across the table, waited until he raised his eyes to hers, and asked tartly, "So what are you going to do about your job?"

Like many victims, Lucas is punishing the people who are trying to help and understand him. Everybody else is out of reach. Such is the wrath of the terrible meek. The idea that being a victim gives them the right to punish others keeps many people firmly stuck in the Victim Trap.

How to Get out of the Victim Trap

If you think the message of this chapter is to stop fixing the blame and start fixing the problem, you're correct. Many of you might be willing to consider that possibility—except that blame is harder to give up than nicotine or chocolate. It can be such a well-ingrained habit that it doesn't seem like a habit at all, just a clear view of reality. Once you decide that something or someone is to blame for what happens to you, this idea becomes as hard to give up as your certainty that the sun rises in the east. It's a fact of your life. It's out of your hands.

Not quite. It just feels that way. Nobody would suggest that the sun also rises in the west, but there are other interpretations of blame situations.

The first step toward getting out of the Victim Trap is recognizing that to blame someone is one of the most harmful things you can do to yourself.

Then you need to switch off your internal "automatic pilot" and examine how you maintain your belief in blame. Think of it as a cassette tape that you play every time you think about the situation. Lucas's tape, for example, says Amanda is underhanded; she is spoiling his chances, and the agency is being unfair. As we will see in the discussion on fairness in chapter 9, the idea of unfairness helps people to maintain the thoughts they need to stay in the Victim Trap.

You maintain your perception of reality by replaying the same internal tape, to the point where whatever is on the tape seems like reality itself rather than a description of it. You see what you expect to see. The more you expect to see it, the more of it you see. What you tell yourself about what happens determines how you feel about it. To get out of the Victim Trap, you need to change your tape. Instead of your old favorites, try playing something new, like the following questions:

- *When I know who's to blame, how will that help me solve the problem?*
- *If everybody agreed that I'm a victim, would I feel any better?*
- *What do I want to happen? Are my thoughts sending me closer or further away from my goal?*

Or simply try saying:

- *Okay, that's over. It's in the past. Now what am I going to do about it?"*

At first, changing the internal tape will make you feel as if you were suppressing the real you and lying to yourself. Sacred Bulls have a way of becoming more real than anything else because they fit so well with people's automatic pilot. Changing the tape, however, is the only way to start flying on your own.

As you rerun your new tape, reality can change. (The only thing that can stand in your way is the stubborn belief that you would rather be right than effective, a notorious Bull that we will deal with in chapter 11.) Changing the tape is not selling out. Although we see forgiveness as an act of self-interest, with more benefit for you than for the person you're forgiving, you don't need to forgive or forget to get out of the Victim Trap. You do need to move on.

Chapter Seven

THE "NICE" BULL
Avoid Conflict at All Cost

*T*he Organization 2000 project is the much-heralded sav-
ior of the company's competitive position in the twenty-
first century. It involves a complex shifting of responsibilities and organizational focus to bring the company in line
with the challenges of the global market.

It is also an ill-conceived mess.

*Stanford should know. He's been the staff person answer-
ing questions for the managers in the field, and he knows
without a doubt that they aren't getting it. This is not what
Dianne, Stanford's boss, wants to hear. This is not what
her boss wants to hear, either. The unwritten rule in the
company is "Give us only good news."*

*Stanford doesn't know what to do. He's given Dianne
some pretty direct hints that there are big problems, but
she doesn't pick up on them. All she wants to see are the
figures that look good—because that's what she wants to
present at her team meetings.*

*Dianne chooses to see the problems as bugs to be worked
out. From Stanford's point of view, if the problem is bugs,*

then they're the size of the Cockroach Who Devoured Cleveland. Dianne just doesn't take his hints or read his figures the way he does. (Her Bull of Denial is standing in the way.)

Stanford feels hopeless. If he makes a big deal about the difficulties, chances are they will be seen as figments of his "negative attitude" rather than as real problems. He doesn't want a conflict with Dianne, even though he has a sick suspicion that if Organization 2000 falls apart, his career will crumble with it—not to mention a lot of other people's.

His only option for warning her, besides subtle hints that don't work, is a direct confrontation. That's more than Stanford is willing to risk. Maybe things will work out better in the next few weeks. Hey, he can always hope.

Stanford decides his only move is to tell Dianne what she wants to hear. He sighs and prepares to spotlight the tiny successes and gloss over the big failures. He puts on a smile and tries his best to be nice.

In most workplaces, people feel a lot of pressure to be superficially friendly, to get along, and to be, well, superficial. On the surface, there's nothing wrong with being "nice." By all means tell people what they want to hear—if that's what you mean. Being nice works—unless you use the smile and happy face to cover conflicts and disagreements simmering below.

Corporate cultures like this exist because businesses are made up of people, and very few people handle conflict well. Some create it where it doesn't need to be. Far more avoid it in any way they can. They listen, they do favors for people, they're sensitive, they're "nice." They put off the problem until later and hope it will go away.

They desperately want to believe that all their niceness will make up for an inability to look someone in the eye and say, "No, I don't agree." They can't stand hurting other people's feelings. They don't know how to deal with the things people say and do when their feelings are hurt.

Their solution is to devise various strategies and even entire corporate cultures that depend on being nice. All of these strategies share a common element: avoiding a small immediate conflict by risking a bigger one in the future. Maybe, they think, they'll beat the odds and the big blowup will never come. Like Stanford, they keep smiling and hope.

Really, it isn't too hard to fool other people with this strategy. We all are more comfortable around nice people. Sometimes you can even fool yourself. A Sacred Bull will tell you that nothing is worse than a fight. Like everything else these Bulls say, it's a setup. You'll get it in the end.

People don't always get along. Unless they are able to settle their differences constructively, the conflicts grow bigger, until eventually they explode. It is the explosions, not the day-to-day settling of differences, that give conflict such a bad name.

CONFLICT-AVOIDERS CREATE CONFLICT

Conflict-avoiders vary in their strategies and levels of sophistication. All of them try to cover their fear and lack of communication skills with being "nice." Their idea of direct resolution of differences is to tell people what they want to hear. They are just trying to avoid unpleasantness. Although they aren't trying to be deceptive or manipulative, sometimes they appear that way to others.

Conflict to them is always negative because they don't know how to make anything positive from it. This is usually because the conflict grows and becomes harder to manage the longer they put off confronting it.

All conflict-avoiders create bigger conflicts by avoiding smaller ones. The least sophisticated form of conflict avoidance is telling *other* people, instead of the person with whom you have the difference.

Tell Someone Safer

Charlotte and Walter are managers in the same department, and she can't stand him. Charlotte thinks Walter is insufferable. He lies, cheats, and probably steals, although she hasn't caught him at it (yet).

Walter is always insinuating—publicly—that Charlotte's team doesn't work as hard as his and that she doesn't know what she's doing. He phrases his jabs as jokes, but everybody gets the point.

Their manager thinks Walter's all right. They're always talking and joking together—while Charlotte is working, she might add. There's a lot she might add. And she does, every night when she comes home from work. After all, she has to tell someone, and it's usually her husband Hank who's nominated.

The other day, for instance, the team was talking about cost control and Walter said, "Obviously some of our departments are overstaffed," and looked right at Charlotte. She thought about saying something like, "Specifically, Walt, which departments do you mean?" But what's the use? He would just come up with some other put-down or, worse, attack her department directly, in the middle of the management meeting. Charlotte decided not to make a big deal of it—until she got home.

Every few days Charlotte has another story about the latest mean, sneaky, or underhanded stunt that Walter has pulled. Hank doesn't particularly enjoy these recitals (to himself he thinks, "Another dinner with Walter") but he listens and tries to be understanding.

Occasionally Hank tries to offer constructive suggestions like "Talk to Walter" or "Say something to your boss." Charlotte sees this as evidence that Hank doesn't know how bad the problem is. If she says anything to Walter, it just makes matters worse. She just has to smile and be pleasant and make the best of it at work. But she has to do something to deal with the stress.

Lately Hank has been losing patience. He's saying, "Why don't you just quit?" even though he thinks she has a good job and they need the money. He just can't stand seeing what this jerk is doing to his wife.

As Hank grows more upset, Charlotte finds herself withdrawing from him and not talking about Walter so much. Now she's on the phone two or three times a week with her friend Joyce.

Charlotte has a difficult time dealing with Walter directly. At work she tries to be nice and cooperative. She tries to handle the conflicts by talking them over with someone safer: Hank, then later, Joyce.

Talking about Walter so often only makes Charlotte more angry. Every time she hears herself say how terrible and unreasonable he is, she believes it more. Yet she is weakening whatever motivation she has for doing something about Walter by dumping it onto her husband and friend. She is also putting a strain on her closest relationships and creating conflicts there because she cannot deal with the one at work.

Charlotte is creating a situation in which she responds by fuming whenever Walter offends her. Her internal processing of the incident has more to do with how she would tell someone else about it than with how she would deal directly about it with Walter.

This means that, on the rare occasion when her facade cracks, she responds with an attack: "You're always implying my group doesn't do any work!" She could say something more productive: "Walter, what exactly did you mean by that comment?"

What Charlotte says is designed for maximum effect said *to* other people *about* Walter. Her comment to him comes out sounding petulant and childish, an easy target. Her outburst is ineffective. Walter does not respond positively to being told, "You always imply my team doesn't do any work." How could he? He is not being asked for anything except to feel guilty. He can feel free to ignore Charlotte's response.

However, the interaction reinforces Charlotte's belief that "I tried talking to Walter directly and it didn't work." Her blowup merely serves as a response for the next time her audience (Hank or Joyce) asks, "Why don't you try talking to him?" She believes she has tried.

Charlotte is not planning this as an overall strategy. The entire structure is the result of her belief that, when Walter makes a critical comment or does something she doesn't like, the best way to handle it is to try to be nice. Charlotte is convinced that no good can possibly come from getting into a conflict with him.

Charlotte is trying to be nice when she doesn't feel nice. If she really could ignore Walter, as she pretends, there would be no problem. She doesn't ignore him, however. She makes him the star of her fantasy life and the subject of her quality-time conversations. This is not being nice; it is being self-destructive. What Charlotte is doing to protect herself from a few difficult conversations is spoiling her life.

The situation could be worse. Charlotte could do herself vastly more damage by choosing a coworker or (God forbid) her boss as the dumping ground for her negative feelings about Walter. If she confided in a coworker, most of what she said would eventually get back to Walter, giving him more reason to make trouble for her and confirming his belief that she is helpless to do anything about it. If she complained to her boss, the boss would decide very quickly that Charlotte is the one with the problem. (Bosses don't like interpersonal conflict either, as we will discuss later in this chapter.)

The only way out of this situation is for Charlotte to deal directly with Walter. Before she can do this, she must recognize that her beliefs—conflict is bad; it's useless to say anything to Walter; I've already tried and it didn't work—are as responsible for her misery as anything Walter does or could do. (For this reason, we have purposely avoided analyzing Walter.)

To feel better, Charlotte doesn't necessarily need to "win" and get Walter to stop his snide comments. All she needs to do, under her own power, is to make it a little more difficult for him to push her around.

Her husband and friend can help. They probably are conflict-avoiders, too. They don't want to hurt Charlotte's feelings so they are "nice" to her. They listen, even if they don't want to, until they lash out in exasperation. Then they probably go to *their* friends and talk about her. (We are tempted to imagine most of the interpersonal conflicts of the world maintained by an endless circle of conflict-avoiders telling other people instead of the person with whom they have a problem. This is a great victory for the "Nice" Bull, but a defeat for everyone else.)

To break the chain, Charlotte's husband and friend have to stop passively listening and start asking, "What are you going to do about it?" They need to say, "Talking to me about Walter does no good. I'm not willing to listen to it any more. I am willing, however, to spend the time with you discussing possible actions and rehearsing what you might say to Walter."

Charlotte's real problem is a lack of skill in dealing productively with conflict. Nobody ever learns this until they have to. In the short run, all other strategies are easier. In the long run, nothing else will do.

Having gone through this cycle with thousands of people (what do you think people talk to their therapists about?), we know that the hard part about breaking the pattern is not learning the skills for dealing with conflict, but believing that you really have to learn them and use them. The "Nice" Bull is large enough to stand in the way of all logic.

THE "NICE GUY" MANAGER

Conflict-avoiding coworkers cause problems, but they seem manageable compared with the havoc a conflict-avoiding boss can wreak.

When David came on board as the new department manager, he charmed the staff with his witty, casual, open-door style. He really listened when people bared their souls during getting-to-know-you sessions. Department members rejoiced. "Finally we have a boss who has time for us. This guy cares."

Soon several people, including Laura, a middle manager, went to David with differing viewpoints on controversial issues. They all left David's office believing David was behind them. True, David never directly said he agreed, but he listened in such a supportive way.

Later Laura realized that, although David listened and understood her concerns, nothing actually changed. He never gave a clear yes or no. His responses were always vague: "I'll certainly think about this." "I'm going to run this by a few people upstairs." "I'll get back to you." It finally dawned on Laura that her boss didn't really agree at all. He was saying no all the time; it just sounded like yes.

Laura decided to go back and talk to David about the mixed signals. Suddenly, the boss with the open-door policy was too busy for a discussion, and asked to reschedule. Somehow the meeting never materialized.

Then Laura noticed that David's manner toward her was changing. He was still friendly when he passed by her desk, but their follow-up session never happened. David was busy; he had a scheduling conflict; he was so swamped that he forgot the time. He always had a reason and was always apologetic about being unable to sit down for a real discussion.

Now Laura is wondering what she did wrong. All she wanted to do was talk to David about a problem.

David's avoidance of Laura has nothing to do with her personally. It is the *conflict* he's avoiding. He hides his fear with his good manners and charm, but the idea of a direct conflict scares him so much that he has to run. He is frightened by the idea of anyone's being angry at him or of his having to hurt anyone's feelings.

Like many managers, David is trapped by the "Nice" Bull. He has few skills in handling conflict. If you asked him about his verbal dodgeball tactics with Laura, he probably would smile, shake his head ruefully, and say, "I just don't know how to say no."

Actually, the word *"no"* is in his vocabulary. What David needs are words to say to *himself*, words that would allow him to tolerate the hurt feelings and anger that saying no often generates, and the motivation to deal with it. There is very little in the system in which he operates to push him toward dealing with conflict. All the short-term rewards are given for dancing away.

Of course, some of the people in David's department already are feeling angry at him, not because of anything he actually said but because of what he *hasn't* done and hasn't said. Like Laura, they think he's unavailable to them because he doesn't like them or is angry at them. If they ask him directly, he will reassure them that he's certainly not angry; he's just so busy. The result is that nothing will change.

THE FIVE WS FOR DEALING WITH "NICE GUY" BOSSES

Learning to deal with conflict-avoiding, dance-away bosses like David involves asking the right questions.

Bosses like this will seldom lie but, unless you ask very direct and specific questions, you may not get the whole truth. The five Ws of journalism may come in very handy:

WHO needs to approve this decision?
WHAT do you think she'll say?
WHEN do you plan to talk to her?
WHERE is she?
WHY don't we go talk to her together right now? (If not now, *WHEN?*)

Keep your tone and the questions as friendly as possible. There is no point in making people run away by accusing them of avoiding you. This kind of boss excels in dancing away, so you need to use your time together to your best advantage.

Even David's boss cannot and will not try to make him change. David's no-conflict management style is one of the most common in business. In most companies it may not be highly rewarded, but this style is rarely punished. After all, the thinking goes, there's no point in asking for trouble. Making deals and turning a profit are worthy challenges for a manager. Dealing with interpersonal unrest is not. Why waste time and energy on people with bad attitudes?

CONFLICT AND CORPORATE CULTURE: IT'S NOT NICE TO GET INVOLVED

Learning effective communication is not a high-priority skill in most companies. Many managers define *communication* as (1) being persuasive, and (2) having sense enough to avoid saying things that will make other people (especially your boss) angry. If you have enough power, you can communicate any way you want. If you don't, you'd better be "nice."

Most people have such a difficult time dealing with conflict constructively that it is suppressed and discouraged in most business cultures. In most workplaces, conflict is viewed as an aberration. Typically, it is interpreted in one of three ways: one person using his power to lord it over another; a power struggle between two people; or somebody with a bad attitude making life miserable for everyone else.

All of these interpretations carry with them a clear message about what you should do when other people are in conflict. Like witnessing a mugging on the street, don't get involved. This is another example of how Sacred Bulls work. They control our behavior by changing our perception of what is going on. The "Nice" Bull can give you a million reasons to stay far away from any trouble you might see.

In many workplaces, the last thing most people would see in a conflict situation is a real issue that might have some substance that requires taking a stand or trying to help get the issue settled. The "Nice" Bull says, "Stay away," and that is what most people do. It's definitely better for your career. At least in the short run.

"The handle falls off when it gets hot." People say it as a joke, and the joke is on Zach in Research and Development. Nobody knows what he's trying to prove. The company stands poised to introduce the first practical cordless hair dryer—a product that will revolutionize the industry and capture a tremendous share of the market—and here's this one guy griping.

Everybody knows why. Zach is so jealous that he can't stand it. This new idea came not from his high-priced department but from some guy who invented it in his garage. The guy wrote a letter to Raul, the CEO, and it's been

Raul's baby ever since. He bought it and has been its chief booster. The company has spent a lot of money already, and Zach is the only one who seems to have a problem. Sour grapes.

Zach's department is the only one with anything invested in the product's going wrong. So they put it through tests and, well . . . "Sure, it falls apart at a zillion degrees. So would I," Raul said at the marketing meeting, and that is the official position.

Really, this is a battle between Zach and Raul. Nobody wants to step between these two heavy hitters. There's no percentage. Most people know Zach is a straight shooter who wouldn't fake a test over sour grapes. But they also know Raul is a good leader with a real eye for something that will sell. Nobody particularly wants to be seen as a troublemaker by asking for more data on the tests.

So for a few weeks the joke is current around the office. When anything goes wrong, people say, "The handle falls off when it gets hot." Very funny.

Until the first customer complaints started coming in.

The results of avoiding conflict can be disastrous, as with the hair dryer. Most often, however, the result of ignoring conflicts is just misery and stress for everyone not agile enough to get out of the way or powerful enough to delegate it to someone else.

Ignoring conflict can do damage. Differences of opinion may yield something productive for the company, but getting involved usually does no one's career any good in the short run. The best corporate politicians are the ones who can put conflict on a back burner, or delegate it, or do anything with it other than deal with it.

Carl sees himself as a diplomat. Everybody else sees him as two-faced. Carl feels there's no point in getting into arguments, so he always agrees with whoever comes to him with a problem. Later, when he thinks no one is paying attention, he tries to make "little changes" to solve the problem. Of course, people feel the effect of his little changes, and resent what they consider his double-dealing. Carl can't understand why everybody is always mad at him, even though he works so hard to keep people happy.

Conflicts are inevitable in any business. They aren't just the result of temporary bad moods. They don't just go away. Managers who avoid conflicts and try to tell everybody what they want to hear often make themselves (and everybody else) miserable.

The goodwill and trust of the people who work with you are essential. "No-problem" management can lead people to believe that they cannot count on you to tell them the truth. Most people would rather deal with a straightforward no than with the "Nice" Bull.

People who do deal directly with conflicts are often seen as grumpy—or worse.

Victoria doesn't like arguments. Her knees feel shaky and her mouth gets dry, but she tells herself that if she doesn't say no now, it will be even more difficult later.

True, some people see Victoria as difficult to deal with. Sometimes they describe her with a word that rhymes with rich. But people do respect her. They agree that, on the whole, they appreciate knowing where they stand. Not everybody likes her, but everybody trusts her.

If you are a manager, the rewards for dealing directly with conflict come mostly in the form of trust from the people below you. Unless you are extremely skilled, you may not win any popularity contests. Your own corporate culture will have to dictate which is more important: trust or popularity.

The J.C. Dithers Approach

Some managers think they are doing a good job of handling conflict when all they are really doing is pulling rank.

Bob is a tough, hard-hitting manager. Among the many things he won't put up with is whining. When people in his department come to him with a conflict, he doesn't avoid it. He tells them who's right and chews them both out for not being able to figure it out for themselves. Everybody back to work!

At management meetings, Bob boasts about how easy it is to handle conflict if you aren't afraid to take a stand.

Actually, Bob's behavior is intensifying the level of conflict in his department. Instead of encouraging people to compromise and work things out, Bob keeps the situation unbalanced by throwing the weight of his authority to one side or the other. His actions leave people with a need to get back at each other. He also has made it an unwritten rule that battles are won by whoever is most effective at manipulating the boss. Bob ends up being a powerful, hard-hitting dupe. He isn't "nice," but he's still avoiding conflict.

Fortunately, most managers are less cavalier in their attitudes about their job. Overconcern with responsibility is a more common pattern.

The Boss Knows Best

Remember the sitcom dads of the '50s? They were calm, caring, self-sacrificing, and reasonable, above petty day-to-day squabbles. When they came home from work, they'd settle everything with a few kind but firm words.

Gee, thanks, Dad. You're the greatest guy since President Eisenhower.

This ideal of masculine nurturance is still alive and well back at the office. It is the model many men (and women) use for being a good manager.

Jim cares about the balance between the demands of production and the needs of his employees. He tries to set an example of positive and constructive behavior. He takes a lot of responsibility for what happens in his department.

When a problem comes up, Jim takes time to think about it. Usually, he decides that the best way to handle it is to take the people involved into his office and share some kind, firm (and heartfelt) words that remind everybody that they can resolve this little dustup in a constructive way. He believes a kind word (and an occasional playful punch on the shoulder) turns away wrath.

Jim is earnest and caring, and his employees feel affection for him. The bottom line, however, is that he is ineffective.

Jim is working with outdated equipment. Kind, firm words may have been enough to calm sibling rivalry on TV in the '50s, but they are not enough to solve the problems of the '90s. Jim's Mr. Nice Guy style sends an unconscious message that there is something wrong with conflict—that it is unconstructive, immature, and dangerous. Much better to sweep it under the rug and be "nice."

After awhile his employees realize that Jim will not actually *do* anything about problems, other than listen carefully and offer an inspiring pep talk. Like the '50s sitcom dad, he is above the fray, but he does not have the moral authority at the office to settle everything with the right lecture in the last five minutes of the show. Nobody ever did in real life.

Life at work is painful for Jim. The problems grow more serious in his department, and he blames himself. Ward Cleaver would have done a better job. Jim knows he just isn't the man he should be.

Sometimes, he admits, he's tempted to blame his employees. He'd like to chew them out for their incessant pettiness and immaturity, but that would be out of character. He never tells anyone. He would feel guilty if he expressed these feelings. He avoids conflict with himself even more often than he avoids conflict with others. If he even admitted to any of these feelings, Jim would feel as petty as the worst of his employees.

Instead, Jim keeps his positive front and holds his anger back, where it bubbles and boils in his gut until he develops that quintessential '50s disorder—an ulcer.

Jim's ulcer is one of the problems that followers of the "Nice" Bull can develop when they are maneuvered by their own beliefs into acting one way on the outside and feeling a different way on the inside.

We are not suggesting that Jim should start throwing tantrums with his subordinates. He does need to look at his anger at and disappointment in them, even if it makes him feel guilty and unworthy.

Jim has to face the conflict with himself before he can deal effectively with the people who work for him. He needs to face the horrible truth about himself—that inside, like all human beings, he isn't really nice all the time. He needs to talk about what he's feeling, to admit it, and to look at it before he can discover how to get beyond it. Behind most unseemly emotions lies not a bad person but one who is making mistakes about or misperceiving what's going on around him.

Jim assumes everyone is as nice as he is. He is disappointed and angry when people don't follow the same rules that he does. He becomes so upset that he doesn't even try to discover what rules they do follow.

As a result, this decent, hardworking guy is effective only as a manager of other decent, hardworking people like himself. To them, a pat on the back or a stern word are more than sufficient. Jim feels comfortable only with people from whom he can remain emotionally aloof.

Other people arouse feelings in him that he would rather not experience. He avoids the guilt of looking at or really experiencing the feelings that could help him understand himself. Instead, he bears the pain of his ulcer and his sense of personal failure rather than be someone who is not "nice."

Guilt and Superwoman

The major conflict nice people try to avoid is with themselves.

Jane is a wonderful, caring person. Ask anyone in her office, her community, or her family. She prides herself on her organization (and she's sure that if she ever lost her weekly planner, her life would be over). Without her superb ability to plan, she would never be able to fit so much productive activity into each day.

She's a manager with a high-tech company, with a good chance of being named department head before too long. Fifty hours is a short workweek for her. She also serves on a couple of nonprofit boards and is helping out a friend's campaign for county commissioner. (She has a wicked backhand, too. You'll see her on the court every Saturday morning, unless her tennis date conflicts with her daughter's softball or soccer schedule.)

Of course, Jane spends quality time with her family and friends. If you'd like to do lunch, she has an opening two weeks from Tuesday, or maybe a walk this Monday at 6 A.M. But if you have a problem and need her help, she'll drop everything and see you now. That's the kind of person Jane is.

She firmly believes that if you are organized and you care about people, you can have it all. Jane has it all. Doesn't she? Then why, lately, has she been feeling a little off? Her energy isn't quite what it was, and she doesn't feel as upbeat as she used to. She senses that something is missing, but she can't possibly imagine what it might be.

Jane takes little pride in being Superwoman. She doesn't see herself as exceptional at all, but as a person who is barely managing to do all the things she has to just to feel like a worthy human being. The real problem is she feels she doesn't have the right to say no to commitments. It isn't nice.

Her increasing tiredness and waning motivation frighten her. If she leaves out something, she will have to confront her own guilt and possibly admit to herself that she doesn't really want to live her life for other people. She may even confess to times when, surrounded by need and obligation, instead of rising to the occasion she'd like to take a nap.

In the long run, the nap would probably do the world more good. Jane would have more to give if she took better care of herself. Of course, if she did stop and rest, she might have to hear the cries of the couch potato within. Worse, she would have to confront feelings of resentment and a desire to have some things in her life that are just for her. She would have to come to grips with feelings she would consider selfish and unworthy. She would rather bend steel in her bare hands.

"Nice" Predators

Nice people can be effective predators. Their favorite weapon is guilt, and their prey is—you guessed it—other nice people. Imagine how much extra work you can get out of someone who feels she shouldn't be asking for anything for herself.

Kelly had based her own management style on Dr. Maxwell, her mentor, a soft-spoken, reserved man of impeccable courtesy. Voices never rose in Dr. Max's domain. Conflict and harsh words seemed to hurt him physically. His face paled, and he would place a hand protectively over his heart. He never demanded; he suggested.

Kelly would do anything to avoid upsetting him. Dr. Max was the nicest person in the world. He was touchingly grateful the day she accepted her new work load without complaint. In addition to her full slate of management duties, he asked Kelly to also take charge of a new, high-profile outreach project, training and supervising student and community participants.

Kelly accepted the challenge. She knew Dr. Max appreciated her team spirit. He looked so guilty when he apologized for burdening her this way, especially when there was no money in the budget for additional compensation. But, he had shrugged helplessly, what else could he do? She was the only manager he could rely on for such an important project.

Kelly handled her double role for eighteen months, taking no lunch hours, working late every night, and bringing work home each weekend. Then she went on maternity leave.

During a long, chatty visit with a colleague, Kelly was shocked to learn that her replacement had laughed at Dr. Max when he outlined the existing terms of the work load. Then, ignoring Dr. Max's piteous cries of distress, she had negotiated a new arrangement. One-third of Kelly's former management tasks were permanently delegated to two subordinates; her replacement was receiving a handsome stipend, in addition to Kelly's full salary, for her work on the outreach project.

Kelly shut the door on her visitor and leaned against the doorjamb, shaking with fury. So this was where being nice had gotten her—unanimous choice for Chump of the Year. She ran to the phone and dialed Dr. Max's office number. She would tell that snake exactly what she thought of him.

Kelly quickly hung up the phone, stunned by her own premeditated rudeness. How could she plan to attack someone for taking advantage of her? How could she have such rude thoughts?

She knew darn well how she could have them. Dr. Max had skillfully used her own guilt to manipulate her, just as other people in her life had done. But this time it will be different.

She knows she won't get anywhere right now by yelling at Dr. Max. When she comes back, however, he will have a different Kelly to deal with, one who can say no and won't take no for an answer. Kelly picked up the phone and dialed again.

HARNESSING THE "NICE" BULL

The biggest damage the "Nice" Bull does to you is to create conflicts within yourself by avoiding them with others. He makes you look at parts of yourself that you'd rather not see. These parts often seem to be so unworthy and evil that we can work ourselves to exhaustion or capitulate forever (or simply dance away) to avoid seeing them.

If we are lucky enough to be forced to look at them, after the initial shock subsides, we see not evil but normal human feelings.

We want things for ourselves and we get upset if other people don't give them. We want other people to think the way we do and we get angry when they don't. When we realize these things about ourselves, conflict becomes easier to deal with because we don't have to do it with one hand tied behind our back.

If we accept ourselves as we are, we are no longer at the disadvantage of having to do all our dealing with others while trying to be someone we're not. We can untie our hand and tie up the Bull.

Most conflict-avoiding, nice people have read books and attended workshops on effective conflict resolution. They keep searching in the vain hope that they will find a technique that is so powerful that it will make conflicts evaporate and they won't have to deal with them.

There is no such technique. Before you can be effective at handling conflicts, you have to know and accept the truth. Conflicts make you feel things about yourself and others that you'd rather not feel. That's why people avoid them.

Widening your definition of yourself unties your hand from behind your back. (While you have the rope out, tie up the Bull of Denial instead.) Then you can give yourself permission to use all the techniques you've read about— or are going to read about here.

IDEAS FOR EFFECTIVE CONFLICT RESOLUTION

Effective conflict-resolution skills are chains of thoughts and actions that are considerably more complicated than smiling, making eye contact, and offering a one-minute reprimand. These skills involve subtlety, sensitivity, and knowledge of how other people think and feel. Count yourself a real communicator if you can handle conflict in ways that keep everybody talking to each other and maintain a trusting relationship.

You can become more effective at handling conflict by asking yourself the following three questions at the first sign of conflict. The real secret is not in what you do but in what you know about your "opponent" and yourself.

1. *"Am I under attack?"* Most of us recognize attacks instantly. Rapid, loud talking, finger pointing, and red faces are fairly clear indicators, but most people also are sensitive to much subtler signs. Some can detect criticism or impending anger at a level of two to three parts per billion.

If you have a tendency to avoid conflict, you can use your own discomfort as a warning light that lets you know you're under attack. Before responding, use this knowledge to figure out exactly how you're being attacked. Is it coming from the other person or yourself? What is going on, and what feelings does it arouse in you? Don't just run away. Figure it out.

2. *"Am I talking with an equal, superior, or inferior?"* With superiors, most people are on their guard. A typical be-nice approach is to tell the boss exactly what she wants to hear while presenting yourself as favorably as possible. What you say becomes less conversation and more presentation. Be most aware of what you want to say rather than what your superior wants to hear. Be sure you know the difference.

People unconsciously use communication shortcuts when dealing with people they consider inferiors. The most common shortcuts are not listening and not responding, often performed with a pleasant smile and glazed eyes. Another be-nice tactic is overexplaining or trying to adopt the "inferior" person's own communication style. The result is condescension.

3. *"What is my goal?"* If somebody is doing something that bothers you, figure out what you want them to do instead. Are you looking for more money? A challenge? A connection with another company? Time off? A chance to do something else? What? Think clearly about what you really want and set your priorities. Know what a successful outcome would be for you. Many conflict-avoiders ignore their own best interests because they are focusing so intensely on avoiding any disagreement.

Wanting to win too much is a good way to lose. Some-times people think they will "win" if they can get the other person to back down. Conflict-avoiders often think of conflict as a win/lose situation. You can use your ten-dency to be nice to your advantage, by picking up on this and appearing to back into the position you wanted in the first place. You may find it's really quite easy to act as if you're backing down. The key is to ask for more than what you want at the beginning.

THE BULL OF PERFECTION
If It's Not Perfect, It's Nothing

*T*he report is in its fourth draft. Happy to be almost finished, Deb shows it to Terry, her boss, for a final check before she goes home.

Terry smiles. His eyes brighten as he picks up his red fountain pen. He lowers his head, grunts, nods, and makes a red mark here and there.

Deb's shoulders relax. Maybe she won't miss dinner after all.

As Terry hands back the report, he shakes his head, more in sadness than anger. "What is here is fine, Deborah — with a few corrections. It seems to me, however, that we have left out a few important details that change the way we present our information. Only the last two sections need some rethinking."

Deb grabs the edge of the desk for support. She counts it up in her head. That's more than twenty pages. "Isn't this a little extreme for a monthly report?" she asks faintly, fanning herself with the rejected pages.

Terry's eyes narrow. "You know the rules around here, Deborah. If it is not perfect, it is nothing."

Terry believes that painstaking attention to detail, hard work, and motivation are the secrets of success. He never misses an opportunity to expound on his creed to his less-experienced (and less-enlightened) coworkers.

He is good at what he does, and he does work hard. Nobody can deny that. But success has eluded him. After twenty years with the same company, he's still a middle manager, though his intelligence, knowledge of the business, and experience should have carried him higher.

The problem is that Terry is such a difficult and demanding person to work for that he is not considered a viable candidate for a higher position. At home he's on his third marriage (and things are a bit rocky there, if office rumors are true). Nobody, it seems, can live up to his standards—least of all Terry himself.

He blames himself for the things that have gone wrong. He should have worked harder. He should have paid more attention to detail. Maybe he could have done a better job at work and at home.

His main consolation is focusing on the details of the job—doing them perfectly. Time sheets, expense accounts, staff memos, even his rough drafts—perfect in every detail. His department's monthly report is always the last to reach the boss's desk, but it's perfect down to the last detail on page 43.

Terry's cardinal rule is, "If it's not perfect, it's nothing." He sees this rule as the secret of all his successes. It is also the source of all his failures.

Vice Masquerades as Virtue

The Bull of Perfection would have you believe that perfectionism is a virtue. He will tell you that perfectionism means:

- Being motivated
- Working hard
- Paying attention to details
- Doing a good job
- Giving more than is asked for

Perfectionism actually means:

- *Being driven*
- *Not being willing to stop working*
- *Being obsessed by details*
- *Doing a job that meets your own standards, regardless of the standards it is supposed to meet*
- *Reducing your own anxiety as the unstated major goal of nearly every task*

Perfectionism is a vice that masquerades as a virtue. Rather than being a quality to boast about, it is a trait you have to monitor closely to prevent the subtle damage it does to your own performance and to your relationships with superiors, coworkers, and subordinates. The Bull of Perfection never knows when to stop, but you need to if you want to keep perfectionism from taking over your life.

If you're not a perfectionist, what we're saying may come as a surprise. Most of us tend to regard perfectionism as a positive trait. We want all the bolts tightened, the figures inputted in the right places, and all the words spelled correctly. Even people who aren't perfectionists have to do important tasks without mistakes. Their motivation is to achieve a positive feeling about their performance. They feel good when they get everything right.

Perfectionists take pride in perfectionism in the abstract. They like to see themselves as the kind of person who takes care of details. They feel good about doing things right, but that feeling is often very short lived. For perfectionists, the main goal is to avoid the negative feelings they get from doing something less than perfectly—or worrying that they might.

The idea that the importance of the task should dictate the amount of effort to expend on it confuses them. *Any* task seems important to them, if doing it perfectly will relieve their anxiety for awhile. The importance of the task to other people may not be much of a factor in deciding how much effort to spend on it.

Perfectionists' internal world is filled with confusion, anxiety, and worry over small details. The only escape comes from doing things perfectly. They will assign equal importance to tasks they do well because the tasks are objectively necessary to the job (writing the monthly report, for example), *and* to tasks they do well as a ritual to calm their own anxieties (opening, reading, sorting, and categorizing the morning mail on their desk).

If you look closely at perfectionists at work, their priorities may seem a little off. From a distance they can look deceptively efficient. In many areas perfectionists seem to see the world in sharper focus than do other people. Details seem larger, and tiny mistakes take on the character of glaring errors. Perfectionists can get the details just right. They have to. If not, the anxiety is more than they can handle. They become addicted to details because getting details right can relieve some of the constant internal pressure. Getting the details right becomes an end in itself, and they lose their view of the big picture.

Hooked on Details

Doing things perfectly can lead to responsibility, achievement, and high-quality work. But it can also lead to lowered productivity, self-disgust, and disruption in relationships with coworkers. When you don't know how to say no to your perfectionist tendencies, the Sacred Bull develops addictive potential.

People tend to hide and deny most other addictions (except for certain developmental periods, as when young males first move into their own apartments and proudly stack all the beer cans they empty). The Bull of Perfection will try to persuade them to flaunt the vice of perfectionism as a virtue.

Todd takes the time to look just right before he steps out the door each morning. His taste is understated, never flashy; you notice the subtle coordination of his shirts and ties with his suits. His car is always right, too, a gleaming navy blue, with never a trace of road dirt or muddy cat footprints that mar the surfaces of the machines of lesser mortals.

Todd's image is perfect; but unless you've been there, you cannot imagine the cost. Worrying about when he can grab half an hour to get to the car wash can distract him most of the morning. Yesterday he begged off a lunch meeting to run down to the cleaners to get his pants pressed.

It bugs him to death if something is slightly off-line. He went completely berserk the day he walked into the parking lot and discovered a ding in the door of his car. He canceled all his appointments to get it to the body shop immediately so he wouldn't have to look at it. Later, when his coworkers teased him, Todd laughed and said, "Yeah, I'm a little bit crazy about things like that." If you listened closely, however, you would have heard a tiny note of pride in his voice.

When something looks wrong, Todd just can't stop worrying about it. He needs to fix the problem before he can think of anything else. If you were to ask him to list his priorities, he would place many things ahead of appearance. But the fact is he puts everything else on hold when his car is dirty or there's a spot on his tie.

Like many perfectionists, Todd doesn't even realize his priorities are out of line. He is just doing what he feels he has to do. It would probably surprise him to see how much time he devotes to having everything look right (you should see his yard at home). Yet he also feels overworked, pressured, and harried—as if there's never enough time to do the things he wants to do.

From the outside, it seems that Todd chooses to allocate so much of his time to appearance because he enjoys having everything look right. He does take some pride in his perfect appearance, but that's nothing compared with the worry he experiences when something looks *wrong*. Much of the time that worry determines what Todd does. Keeping the anxiety under control by having everything perfect is his highest priority—and he doesn't even realize it.

The Bull of Perfection may try to convince you that perfectionism is a positive trait, a boon to mankind. If you follow the Bull, you'll discover it's more like a lifelong game of catch-up. Of course you know that nothing is perfect, yet you still have to try for perfection—not because you want to but because you have to. No partial credit allowed, either.

PERFECT, OR IT'S NOTHING

The addictive part of perfectionism is not, as many would suppose, a feeling of superiority. Others may think perfectionists are always congratulating themselves for how much they do and how great they look. Not true. Perfectionists do get a feeling of achievement and, perhaps, sometimes even superiority for a little while when everything is going right—but that feeling is fragile and fleeting. Something, of course, always goes wrong, which forces the perfectionist to have to catch up.

When you're a perfectionist, you don't feel that you

have many choices. You're just doing what you have to do.

You can lose touch with priorities—your own and those of the people you work for and with. The Bull of Perfection says it's okay not to count all the time you spend trying to achieve perfection in your chosen area. Everybody else *is* counting, however.

It's Perfect, and It Takes Forever

The biggest problem for all perfectionists is perspective and priorities, because they are afraid of the anxiety they would have to face if they did something halfway. Perfectionists are always in danger of spending more time on minor details than on the important tasks.

In law school, Courtney was rewarded lavishly for her perfectionism; she was graduated first in her class. Her papers were masterpieces of detail and always included all sides of an issue. Her research was impeccable and exhaustive. Her briefs were—well, not brief. Courtney's classmates teased her by saying she could save money by subletting her apartment and moving into the law library, since she seemed to spend most of her hours there anyway. She was proud of the teasing.

The work was hard in law school, but Courtney could do it exactly the way it needed to be done. She had no other demands on her time, and she didn't need much sleep. The teasing and the perfect grades were evidence that she was doing it right. She felt in control.

It has always taken her forever to put out a product. In law school she would go through eight or nine drafts before she felt ready to hand in her work. She knew she could include more references, her language could be clearer, and she would perpetually find mistakes. Her work was excellent, but it took an enormous amount of time to produce.

Nevertheless, it got her through law school at the top of her class.

Now Courtney is working for a prestigious law firm, and her style has given her a great deal of trouble. As always, she takes a long time to put out a product. Her clients have begun to complain about the delays; they just want a contract, not a brief for the Supreme Court.

She is giving them far more than they asked for because that is the minimum she is comfortable with. Her clients are concerned that all the time it takes to produce these masterpieces is going on their tab. But Courtney isn't gouging them by any means. Often she is embarrassed to put down the number of hours she spends on one case because her time is so far out of line for the work accomplished. Although she still works her long hours, her billables aren't too great.

Though Courtney's work is of excellent quality, the partners see her productivity as mediocre. Worse, she's always so busy that she doesn't have time to politick them for the really good, career-advancing cases. She takes what she's given and does the best job she can by her own standards— and she expects everybody else to meet those standards, too. She has become the prime topic of lunchtime gossip among the secretaries and paralegals whom she has terrorized and humiliated for tiny mistakes.

Courtney feels perpetually overwhelmed. Inside, she is convinced that she takes so much longer to do things because she is not as bright as her peers. She feels she has to substitute hard work and attention to detail for other people's superior abilities. Her friends keep nagging her about her nonexistent social life. Well, maybe other people can balance playtime and a career; but for her, there's no way. The work is always piling up, and she's always kicking herself for being behind.

Already the first of the people who were hired in her year has made partner. Nobody's even mentioned a time line for partnership for Courtney. She's distraught. It feels like an

F, the first she's ever gotten. She feels terrible about herself and tries to make up for her failure in the only way she knows: She vows to work even harder.

Courtney is probably the brightest person in the law firm, but her perfectionism is crippling her in several ways. Her attention to detail keeps her from finishing her work on time. Her own standards are far beyond what is demanded by her clients or the firm. Unlike her professors, they don't give her a better grade for doing a little extra. They get upset with how much time and effort she spends on even the simplest task.

Courtney has always regarded her time as her own. She could use as much of it as she wanted to indulge her perfectionism. Now the firm regards her work time as theirs, and she is not using it wisely. They want her to take on more cases, do them reasonably well but not perfectly, finish them on time, and be ready to take on new cases.

Her work style and her lack of attention to law-firm politics is holding back Courtney's career. The worst problem, however, is the one going on inside. It is the way Courtney motivates herself. If the partners told her what she tells herself, they would be called abusive and accused of harassment. Courtney regularly maligns herself for being stupid, lazy, and inefficient. She sees her job and her life as an enormous, losing game of catch-up. She believes that the only way to make things better is to work harder, which is what she did in law school. The strategy worked then, but it doesn't work on her job.

Courtney feels out of control and in a panic, and she has no one to blame but herself. She heaps on the abuse to get herself to work harder, but she is already working as hard as she can. The real problem is her own internal inability to let details go. To Courtney, *every-*

thing, rather than the demands of her firm or her clients, is top priority.

She has always pushed herself to take care of the details as a way of managing her anxiety, but that strategy is making her situation worse. Courtney cannot see any of this. She believes her problem can be summed up in two words: *lazy* and *stupid*.

EVERYTHING Is Top Priority

Like everyone else, perfectionists are looking for a feeling of self-worth. For them, self-worth comes from what they do—taking care of details—rather than what they are. Their egos have no "swim bladder" so, like sharks, they have to keep moving to avoid sinking to the bottom of the sea. To stay afloat, they work harder and take care of more details.

Often, like Todd and Courtney, perfectionists lose sight of their priorities because of their attention to detail. What they do to avoid the anxiety caused by minor mistakes creates major mistakes. Their anxiety goes up more and more, and they try to keep it under control by working harder.

Most perfectionists are workaholics by default. There just aren't enough hours in the day to get everything done. The Bull of Perfection tells them that the way to deal with problems is to "work hard and don't make mistakes."

Of course, that is not a totally bad rule. Perfectionists are responsible for many achievements, important and unimportant. The key is that they sometimes cannot tell the difference. Perfection becomes the minimum acceptable standard, which makes it a game no one can ever win. Perfectionists are so busy that, like Courtney, they lose perspective. They set priorities but somehow everything ends up being a 10 on a 1-to-10 scale. The result is they are left with no priorities at all.

A Feeling of Control

To be psychologically healthy, people need a feeling of control over their lives. Despite their obsession with order and details, perfectionists are out of control. The Bull of Perfection is running their lives. They don't see that their central problem is trying to reduce their anxiety by taking care of details. They see this as their major virtue, which is why they do more of it when they run into trouble. They pride themselves on how well they do things, and berate themselves mercilessly when they make a mistake.

A Sense of Challenge

To be psychologically healthy, people also need a feeling of challenge. Considering all the work they do, you'd think perfectionists would have plenty of challenge in their lives. Sheer amount of work completed, however, is not the same as challenge. Their jobs and their lives can end up being an endless chain of details to take care of. Often perfectionists are too busy or too frightened to take on real challenges that might help them get a clearer focus on their priorities. Many perfectionists do not accomplish as much as they could because they let opportunity pass them by or they take on small tasks in preference to the bigger, riskier ones.

Connection to Others

The third element people need to feel psychologically healthy is a sense of connection to other people. Perfectionism does its worst damage in this area. Perfectionists drive themselves. They are demanding, abusive, and punitive if they don't meet their own internal standards. Naturally, they think this is the way to get the best work out of others as well.

PERFECTIONISM CAN PRODUCE SHODDY WORK

When people call themselves perfectionists, it can be hard to tell whether they're bragging or admitting a shortcoming. To them, perfectionism means working hard and driving themselves to produce the best possible product. What could be wrong with that? In fact, they believe if everybody were more of a perfectionist, the world wouldn't be so full of shoddy work. Actually, the Sacred Bull of Perfection is responsible for much of the shoddy work. Here's how it happens.

Jay accepts only the best from himself and his employees—which means that he criticizes everything. If you do something for Jay that's 99 percent right, he will focus on the 1 percent that's wrong. That is the way he treats himself, so he feels justified in making the same demands on others.

Mistakes are unacceptable; they're crimes, in fact. Jay believes he has to punish severely, or people will become repeat offenders. If they allow themselves to make small errors, they will let themselves make big ones. Jay will not tolerate this kind of thinking. It is his duty to nip it in the bud.

Kevin is a demon for getting things done. The people who work with him are amazed at how many balls he can keep in the air and how much he can accomplish. Occasionally he drops one of the balls and makes a mistake. In the overall scheme of things, his mistakes are minor—to everyone but Jay.

Jay chews Kevin out for minor mistakes. During perfor-

mance reviews Jay always says that Kevin should be paying more attention to details. When Kevin, in his own defense, tries to point out how much he gets done, Jay seems unimpressed. "That's what you're paid to do, and you need to do it more carefully," Jay says flatly. He is constantly checking up to see that Kevin is taking care of details. As a result, Kevin's overall organization suffers. He makes more mistakes, not fewer, because of Jay's "help" in attending to details.

In most other settings, Kevin would be a star. In Jay's department, he's usually one step away from probation. No wonder he's looking for a different job.

Perfectionists like Jay can drive away very talented employees because they cannot accept people who have different styles of work from their own—even when the different styles are more productive and get the job done better. Perfectionists can overlook a lot of positive contributions and lock in on details that are much less important.

Jay prides himself on his writing ability. He thinks all written work in his department should have professional "flow." He pays less attention to content than style, hates run-on sentences, dangling participles, and split infinitives, and (go figure) will not tolerate contractions and abbreviations. He will sample written work from all levels of his department and hold it up for several days while he edits it. He usually returns it for rewrite, covered with red marks.

Jay's department has a reputation for taking forever to get work out. Letters to customers and suppliers are delayed. As they focus on good grammar rather than good work, the people in Jay's department are letting some more important things slide.

The result is that Jay hands out a lot of punishment but

no praise. After all, if people get bigheaded, they won't be as careful. Most of his conversations with his employees (and his family and himself) involve telling people what they are doing wrong. Very few people in his department have escaped one of Jay's chewing-outs.

His employees think he's a tyrant. They believe that no matter what they do he will criticize them, so why bother trying to please him? They certainly are not inspired to go the extra mile for him. (They would, however, detour much farther than that to avoid him.) Some even do little things to get back at him—things that can't be traced.

Most of his employees are so focused on avoiding the things that might cause Jay to notice them that they don't pay enough attention to their jobs. Mistakes happen. In Jay's department, they happen with annoying frequency. Jay thinks the problem is motivation. He can't see that the major motivating factor in his department is his own punitive strategy for achieving perfection.

It is difficult to estimate how many mistakes one perfectionist can create. (For someone like Jay, the total may approach six figures.) The irony is that Jay recognizes the mistakes but doesn't see who really caused them. He has simply delegated his mistakes to his whole department. The department's performance is sliding.

Jay is not a happy person. He feels trapped. He would like to be more positive with the people who work for him. He has attended workshops on positive management and knows that he should do more praising. But the errors and mistakes are so glaring that he has to take care of them to keep them from happening again. As a result, he doesn't get around to praising anybody.

He doesn't feel like a tyrant; he feels more like someone who is profoundly misunderstood. Jay believes he has to stand firm or things will get worse. He is not demanding anything from others that he wouldn't do himself. He feels he cannot trust anyone to understand things from his point of view or to pay attention to what he wants. So Jay just clamps down all the harder, which continues to turn his department into a perfect mess.

WHY PERFECTIONISTS MAKE POOR MANAGERS

Perfectionists may be very hard workers but they are seldom effective managers. Because they cannot trust themselves not to make a mistake, they certainly cannot trust anybody else, especially when the stakes are high.

Perfectionists can't avoid the temptation to micromanage. When the pressure is on, perfectionists tend to try to control the process—*how* people do things rather than what they do. Perfectionists see too much danger in allowing people to get results in their own way. There is too much freedom in the process, so perfectionists try to control it all.

They see all differences in performance as differences in motivation. Perfectionists share a common belief with much of the business world, namely, that motivation is an internal property, like intelligence and honesty. They believe that people who are motivated get things done; people who make mistakes aren't motivated enough to do things right. The truth is simpler. Most people will do more of whatever is rewarded and less of everything when they are regularly punished.

Perfectionists seldom use praise. They actually believe in praise, but they praise only what is perfect and there's not much of that around. To a perfectionist, a small mistake stands out like a cigarette billboard in a national park.

Impatience plus perfectionism may equal employee abuse. Impatient perfectionists often have difficulty controlling their temper. In their heads they are always replaying the Sacred Bull's bellow, "You could be doing this better! If it's not perfect, it's nothing!" The result is that people who work for perfectionists tend to feel unappreciated and under attack—and they fight back, passively or actively. They make mistakes, they forget, they do things halfway, and they criticize. Of course, this alarms the perfectionistic manager, who may feel the need to take even more control. Need we say that this only makes the situation worse?

It's hard to talk to a perfectionist about problems. Perfectionists do not accept praise because they know that what they did is not perfect. They do not accept suggestions because they see suggestions as disguised criticism, which means they did something wrong.

How to Work with a Perfectionist

It is much more difficult to work with a saint than to be one. The following suggestions may help you work more effectively with the perfectionist in your office, even if the perfectionist is *you*.

Don't argue about being a perfectionist. Perfectionists may acknowledge that perfectionism is a fault. Inside, however, they probably think it's a virtue (no matter how much evidence you offer to the contrary).

Be as direct and specific as possible about what you want. Don't focus on what the perfectionist did wrong. Don't say, "You never praise me. All you do is criticize me." Ask for what you want the perfectionist to do rather than explain what he or she did wrong.

If you want evaluation, ask the perfectionist to evaluate specific things for specific purposes. "Does this report present the product in a favorable enough light?" "Are my sales totals acceptable?" If you ask general questions

("Am I doing a good job?"), the perfectionist is apt to get hung up on some detail (your taste in clothes, for example) and let that, rather than the overall quality of your work, determine his answer.

Don't ask a question whose answer requires seeing the big picture. Perfectionists are detail people and are more apt to deliver what you want if you can ask for it in detail. (You might try asking for a list of the things you're doing right.)

If you're angry, say so. Don't try to make your point by such indirect methods as making mistakes, withdrawing, avoiding issues, or grumbling to friends and coworkers. Express your anger directly but constructively. Talk about what you feel or what you want, rather than what the perfectionist did.

Ask exactly what the perfectionist wants you to do. Ask for specifics. Make sure you also get a clear deadline for the task. Also find out if you have control over how you accomplish the goal. (This will help you later in the project, when the perfectionist may step in and try to control the process.) If you want to maintain your credibility, meet your deadline.

Expect anxiety attacks when things don't go right. Hostility attacks are common, too. When they happen, don't say something like, "Calm down; it isn't important." In this situation, perfectionists are most vulnerable (or most dangerous). They often cannot tell the difference between reassurance and an attack. Ask, "What would you like me to do?" Then do it if you think it's appropriate. Or say, "I won't be able to do that, but I *will* do [a more appropriate action]."

Don't try to make the perfectionist feel better. That's not your job. Reassurance from you risks starting the "I'm a bad person," "No, you're not" conversation (the nearest thing to perpetual motion known to psychological science). Just say, "You're great," and go do something else.

THE PROBLEM WITH PERFECTION

Remember Courtney? She had been at the top of her law school class. Now she's at the bottom of the list to make partner because of the endless hours she spends taking care of unnecessary details.

Courtney was convinced that she was just too stupid to make partner. All she could think of to save herself was to work harder, which just seemed to make things worse. This morning two clients had yelled at her for holding up their contract because of her "damned nit-picking."

She wearily dropped her briefcase, sank into her chair, and glanced down at the desktop. A bright yellow note from Scott, the managing partner for personnel, said, "See me immediately."

Here it comes, Courtney thought as she trudged to his office.

Scott skipped the pleasantries and pointed to a chair. His voice was brisk. "Courtney, sit down. I have two things to tell you, and I'm not going to mince words. I hope you hear them both.

"First, you are the most talented young attorney this firm has hired in years. Second, if you don't do something about your performance, we're going to have to let you go."

Courtney turned pale and half rose from her chair, but Scott waved her down. "Now, before you decide to start cleaning out your desk, remember the first thing I said. You are a talented attorney and can be a real asset to the firm. This talk we're having today is not the end. I hope it's a beginning. This is what the firm hopes, too."

Scott smiled for the first time. "I think between us we can come up with some ideas to get your career back on track. It won't be easy, but I'm convinced it can be done. It's up to you, though. To begin with, you have to accept that you have a problem."

Courtney sat, silent, her stomach clenching, as Scott

173

continued. "You have a choice of walking out of here and trying to make a go of it at another firm. I think if you make that choice you'll just end up going around in the same circles there."

Courtney nodded. She'd been thinking the same thing herself. Her stupidity and laziness would show up wherever she worked.

Scott went on, "You're probably thinking your problem is that you don't work hard enough or you're lazy, or something like that. That's not it at all."

Courtney blinked, then stared at him. Of course, that was her problem. What else could it be?

"The real problem," Scott said slowly, "is your perfectionism. You're so scared to let the tiniest detail go by that your perspective is gone. Everything's a ten on your priority list." As Courtney listened, dazed, Scott went through a list of her recent cases, pointing out the ones on which she had spent too much time doing a perfect job.

Despite her fear, Courtney was impressed. Scott had really done his homework.

He smiled again. "Now you're probably wondering what the alternative is. You're saying to yourself, 'So perfectionism is bad. What am I supposed to do? Just slap things together and not worry?'"

Courtney nodded worriedly.

Scott's voice was reassuring. "Of course you should care about your work. In its place, perfectionism can be a real asset, to you and to this firm. We know you pay attention to detail. You have the internal motivation to do things right, not because we always demand it of you but simply because doing the job well feels good."

Courtney did not trust herself to speak. She was afraid she might cry. Finally somebody understood.

Scott continued firmly, "But Courtney, the real opposite of perfectionism isn't sloppiness. Efficiency is its opposite. Efficiency means making the most from the fewest possible resources.

"The more you drive yourself crazy—and, I might add, drive the poor paralegals and secretaries you've terrorized to the brink of madness," he smiled to erase some of the sting, "the less you or they actually accomplish."

Shaken, Courtney stared at the carpet, her mind whirling. Scott was challenging some of her most deeply held beliefs. What he was saying was scary, but she had to admit it made sense, too. She still didn't see, though, why he was wasting all this effort on a loser like her.

"Another thing, Courtney," Scott broke in on her reverie. "You're probably wondering why I'm willing to make the effort to work with you. I said you were the most talented attorney we've hired in years. Twenty-five years ago I was a talented kid myself and, like you, I nearly blew my chances because of my perfectionism. George Hilliard—the Old Man himself—took me aside and had a conversation like this with me. Scared me to death, but I got the message. I owe that man, and I'm trying to pay him back."

Scott stood up. "Think about it, Courtney. I know you don't jump into things. If you're willing to put some effort into it, I think we can turn things around for you. Let me know by, say, Tuesday."

Courtney stopped staring at the carpet and wiped a tear away. She took a breath, stood up, and extended her hand for a shake. She didn't have to wait until Tuesday. "I'm in, Scott."

How to Get the Bull off Your Back

Perfectionism can be a positive trait or it can nearly ruin your life. The outcome depends on whether you ride the Bull or it rides you. The difference is your ability to get off. To keep your perfectionist tendencies in check, you must develop ways to tolerate anxiety—without taking destructive action to fix the situation.

On some low-priority tasks, all the details don't need

to be checked. This will help your long-term efficiency, but it may arouse your short-term anxiety. Many perfectionists can't believe that doing things perfectly is their strategy for anxiety management—until they try to stop. Recognize that you'll be doing some worrying and fretting, and have a plan for it. Exercise, relaxation tapes, yoga, meditation, or calling friends who have agreed to listen can all help you get through your withdrawal period.

The following are ideas to help you maintain your perspective and priorities, even when things start going wrong.

Understand that you are as responsible for the problems you cause as for the outstanding achievements you produce. Responsibility means doing something about the problems, not just kicking yourself after you make a mistake.

Know your goal. Every task is part of a larger goal. Ask yourself, "Am I doing this just to be perfect, or is there some larger purpose here?" If there is a larger end, ask how important this task is to achieving it. If you're just doing it to be perfect, cease and desist.

If you're worried that something is not perfect, ask yourself, on a 1-to-10 scale, how important is it? If it's not a 9 or a 10, leave it and tolerate the anxiety. This, of course, depends on the culture of your company. In some companies (those run by perfectionists), attention to detail is blown out of proportion. Look at what successful people are doing and try to do the same. If everybody were going after the 2s and 3s, you wouldn't be having a problem (but your company might).

Pursue something more difficult. The pursuit, not the consummation, of any task is the part that gives people joy and satisfaction. Set bigger, more important goals (such as getting in shape, learning a new skill, or driving Sacred Bulls out of your life).

Set a time limit for a task. Many perfectionists take forever to do things. Set a limit based on the importance of the task. When the time is up, turn in your work no matter what.

Keep trying new things. Let yourself be a beginner. Trying new things again and again will help you deal with anxiety over making mistakes. (You may also realize that making mistakes is a great way to learn how to do things better.)

Be grateful for criticism. Try to get some criticism every day. Then use it. (Also, see chapter 2, on denial, for ways to use criticism productively.)

Use praise as your only means of motivation. Forget about punishing or pointing out mistakes. Reward people for what they're doing right rather than criticizing them for what's wrong. (*You* are included among these people.)

As a manager, set a product and a deadline for people to achieve. Allow people control of the process by which they reach the product. Tell them what you want, then let them decide how to get it to you.

A PERFECTIONIST LEARNS TO CHANGE

Courtney never dreamed she could improve her performance at the firm by spending less *time there, but that's what happened. She had been spending much of her time on the unfocused checking of details rather than on really productive work. Scott worked with her on setting time limits for her tasks according to their importance. (He actually made her use a kitchen timer.) This approach made her much more productive. Now she has some time after work to join a health club and take a class in Japanese (she'd always wanted to but could never find the time). She's even been out on a few dates!*

177

The secretaries and paralegals think Courtney's a changed woman. She asks their opinion now instead of chewing them out. She is also going after, getting, and doing a great job on bigger and more important cases. She's developing a reputation for incisive thinking rather than for the perfect execution of the tiniest tasks.

POSTSCRIPT:

Courtney made partner. It took awhile. In many ways it was harder than law school. Scott was supportive but very tough on her. His interest was to teach her to be efficient and to recognize the firm's priorities, which necessitated downplaying her prodigious ability to attend to detail.

"Believe me, Courtney," he said about a million times. "You can't impress me by throwing that Bull around."

Chapter Nine

THE BULL OF FAIRNESS
I Don't Need to Negotiate for What I Want—I Just Want Fairness!

N eale, an account executive, received a dubious distinc-
tion when Kate was promoted to management during
a hiring freeze at the advertising agency. Neale was assigned
responsibility for all of Kate's open accounts, in addition
to his own work, for the next nine months, until the agency
could hire a replacement for Kate. They told him it was a
good career move. Neale thinks somebody probably said
the same thing to the captain of the Titanic.

As he struggled with his double duties, Neale had to let
some of his own projects slide. But he was certain his boss
would understand and appreciate his efforts. After all, he
was doing the work of two people.

At the end of the nine months, however, Neale found
himself in serious trouble. Instead of offering praise and a
raise, his boss put on the pressure. Neale had neglected to
bring in enough new accounts of his own during the time
he was filling in for Kate. His own sales were down; therefore, his job was on the line.

Angry and hurt, Neale could not believe the unfairness

of his boss's reaction. He had taken it for granted that his work would be recognized and appreciated. Later, however, he realized that, strictly speaking, the boss was right: He had not brought in enough sales. Neale also saw, too late, that he had neglected to lay a key piece of groundwork as soon as he was told to pick up Kate's work load as well as his own. Fair or not, the only thing that had always mattered to his boss was results. Neale had failed to protect himself by negotiating, up front, the terms of his double responsibilities.

Neale's idea of fairness was, "I'll work as hard as I can, and if I don't get all the work done, you'll understand and reward the effort, not the results." When he looked at it this way he could see that his boss would never go for a deal like that. The trouble was that he didn't look at what he was expecting until his job was on the line. At least Neale recognized how he had misperceived the situation while there was still time to do something about it.

Many people never realize that the essence of being successful in business is the ability to arrange deals that each participant perceives as beneficial. Expecting fairness may prevent you from looking clearly at the deal you're offering, to see if someone might actually accept it. Of course, the only way to know if it's acceptable is to go ahead and make your offer, before you do anything else. This is what *negotiating* is all about.

NEGOTIATING: THE ESSENTIAL SKILL

Negotiating is the essential skill for getting what you want in business. It is also the very thing the Bull of Fairness will prevent you from seeing. If you believe there is some cosmic rule book that describes how people are supposed to be treated, you're apt to be very disappointed.

Most of us are far too sophisticated to admit that we believe in fairness. We are likely to shrug our shoulders and say, "Well, what did you expect? Life's not fair" (especially when we're talking about *someone else's* problem). If other people treat us in a way we consider unfair, however, we feel hurt, taken advantage of, and betrayed. As Neale discovered, this Bull is hard to see until he's already run over you.

Kim, a social worker, has been told that she needs to be "more in tune with agency politics." She knows she occasionally gets into squabbles with people over what needs to be done, over the demands of her job and the needs of her clients. The agency rules say that certain things have to be done, and Kim is just asking that they be done that way.

What is this "politics" stuff? It's totally unfair of her boss to make a comment like that, especially considering how busy Kim is. What does he mean, anyway? Does he expect her to let people walk all over her and her clients?

Kim is about to do battle again, this time with her boss. She does not understand that sensitivity to agency politics means recognizing the value of playing the game and getting along.

Kim needs to recognize that her boss is her customer and he is trying to tell her something important about what he needs from her. Her boss does need to be more specific, but Kim needs to back off and listen. She needs to look at some of her actions and try to decide what her boss means. She could mention specific examples and ask, "Is this politics?" Or she could ask for guidance about how to handle a situation.

Thinking or talking about fairness only makes you feel more persecuted. What you really want is a clearer idea of what is required. *Ask.* Then discuss whether the specifics are possible. If you are being asked to do something that you think you cannot do, clarify this concern. The issue of fairness will only get in your way.

Kim *should not*, however, ask specifically what her boss means by "politics." When people say you don't understand politics, they mean you are making someone angry at you (usually the person who's talking to you) because you are not acting in accordance with the unwritten rules.

If Kim directly asks, "What is politics?" she is asking the boss to write the rules. Bosses *should* do this, but most don't. Therefore, the burden is on Kim to examine her own behavior. Attacking, accusing, and making demands on her boss is probably exactly what he means by "politics." Kim will not solve her problem by demanding clarification. Her boss probably thinks she is too demanding already.

DEMANDING FAIRNESS IS AN AGGRESSIVE ACT

You may not realize that searching for (or demanding) fairness for yourself is an aggressive act. Aggression does not mean yelling and screaming. It means imposing your will on your environment. This is essential for getting things done, but it does boil down to insisting that other people accommodate your desires or give something they have to *you*. This is what making deals is all about.

Some people have a hard time looking another person in the eye and asking for the deal they want. Often they find this behavior difficult because direct negotiating calls for more aggressiveness than they feel they have. The Bull of Fairness can lead them to avoid an uncomfortable behavior—being directly aggressive—by substituting another that other people often consider even more aggressive and more offensive.

Often people use the concept of fairness as a way to disguise their aggressiveness from themselves. Instead of asking directly for what they want, they seem to be saying, "I'm just asking for what's rightfully mine. I shouldn't have to make a deal to get it." Needless to say, other people may consider this a bit presumptuous. They may decide to retaliate, or simply to see the person as demanding—which may come as a shock to someone who thinks he's simply asking for what's rightfully his.

The more people hide their aggressiveness, the more annoying it is to everyone else.

Here it is—Tyler's big chance, his dream job. The department head is retiring. Tyler has been working and waiting for twelve years to get this shot. He knows he's the most qualified person; nobody understands the department the way he does. And, for sure, nobody works harder around here. The whole staff is behind him, and that means a lot to him. Tyler knows that if there is any fairness in this world, he's a shoo-in.

If Tyler stops here, he won't get the job. He will have to make a deal directly. He can't count on goodwill for the services he has already rendered to get him what he wants. If he does, he's bound to be disappointed.

The people making the decision are from headquarters and don't know much about the department's needs. They do know that they like their managers to have political savvy, a glimpse of the Big Picture, and a lot of the "Vision Thing." This means a good deal of aggressiveness in being able to promote yourself, get your ideas across, and do what it takes to get what you want. Tyler's management style is more low key; he prefers to quietly see that everybody does the best job possible.

Tyler knows he's facing the biggest sales job of his career. Until now he hasn't had to sell himself or his ideas. Everybody knew him, and his competence just shone through. This time, simple competence won't cut it. Tyler will have to do something new and more aggressive or he won't realize his dream. He can't remember ever feeling this scared.

Unfortunately, a lot of other people are not as perceptive as Tyler. Instead of seeing what they want from their jobs and what they have to do to get it, they see a huge Bull. This creature assures them that other people should already know what they want and be happy to give it to them, without their having to ask directly.

Cassie is always concerned that work be distributed correctly between Accounting and Bookkeeping. Cassie is an accountant, and she clearly knows the difference between tasks that require an accountant's skill and professional training and those that require a bookkeeper's semiskilled number crunching.

Cassie seems to be the only person in the office with the ability to make this important discrimination, however. Her boss is totally insensitive to the line between accounting and bookkeeping. He keeps giving her inappropriate tasks, which she passes on to Bookkeeping, creating a bottleneck there while leaving herself free to do the important accounting work.

Cassie wants to be seen as important and highly skilled, as is her due—in her view. The view from her boss's seat is that Cassie is a lazy pain in the posterior.

Compensation is the most common area for discussion of fairness. "Equitable pay" usually means "I think I should be making more money."

Molly and Ira agree that their job is the most difficult in the department. They have to do all kinds of real work—unlike Claire, their boss, who spends all her time shuffling papers and going to meetings. If things were fair in this company, Molly and Ira would make at least twice as much as Claire does (and probably more).

Claire is uncomfortable with compensation in her department. After all, she's in a management position that re-

quires an MBA, yet her salary is barely above that of a few of the more senior workers in the department—Molly and Ira, for example. A greater salary differential would be more fair, Claire thinks, in view of all the training and expertise her job requires.

All of the people in these examples have used the concept of fairness to blind them to the fact that they are making demands in their own self-interest. If they are asking only for what any right-thinking person would realize they deserve, they don't have to give anything back for it. The debt is already paid. They don't even have to say please. They are righting a wrong rather than asking for what they want. They are being reasonable, while the people who assign work to them or decide what they are to be paid are being unreasonable.

With the concept of fairness, you not only never have to say you're sorry, you never have to say, "I owe you one," either. Needless to say, this does not seem fair to the people around you. They see what you're doing as either an attack to be defended against or as an unreasonable demand to be ignored. If you ask for fairness, you are apt to get nothing except the anger of the people around you.

So what do you do?

Be clear about what's going on. We suggest that you throw out the concept of fairness (at least to describe other people's dealings with you) and *start asking for what you want*. Then *be prepared to negotiate*. (What you'll get is usually what you can negotiate.) Everything has a price.

If the World Is Fair, Everything Is Clear

The Bull of Fairness magically eliminates ambiguity by making clear communication someone else's responsibility. Ambiguity is one of the most frustrating parts of anyone's job. Communication is seldom clear, and expectations are never completely spelled out. The Bull of Fairness will tell you that it's up to someone else to resolve the ambiguity. If you expect someone to come along and explain to you what's actually going on, a lot of opportunities will pass you by and a lot of troubles will overtake you.

As we emphasized in chapter 4, the people you work for and work with are your customers. To get what you want you have to give them what they want. That kind of transaction is the simple basis for all business.

Whether you like it or not you are in business for yourself. The more you recognize that the world is your customer, the more competitive you can be. The idea of fairness turns this relationship around and makes you feel as if *you* were the customer to be satisfied. You have a right to this perception, of course, but it will give you little but heartache, resentment, and the compulsion to keep making the same mistakes. This is the sort of trap Sacred Bulls can set for you, traps that are guaranteed to keep you wondering why things never work out right.

Often what people want from you is not completely clear. If a request is so vague that you can't figure it out, you may feel frustrated and angry. (Maybe your boss has asked you to "improve your attitude" or "be more of a self-starter" or make fewer mistakes.) The vague request may be unfair, but calling it unfair won't get you anywhere. You need to figure out what the other person is asking for—especially if the other person is your boss.

If It Hurts, It Isn't Fair

The Bull of Fairness may prompt you to use the fact that a task may hurt you to convince yourself that it isn't fair that you should have to do it. In many jobs people legitimately are asked to do things that may harm them.

The possible harm may be physical, such as putting out a fire or lifting heavy objects, or emotional, such as laying off someone you like or going along with an order with which you disagree. Even if you can ask to get out of it, avoiding the pain might not be best for anyone.

Beth doesn't think it's fair that she should have to fire Marilee. True, Beth is the office manager of the department and Marilee has not been coming in regularly since she was hired. But Marilee is her friend, and Beth knows how hard things are for Marilee, especially since her divorce.

Marilee has a lot of health problems that nobody seems able to diagnose. One doctor thinks she has Epstein-Barr virus although it doesn't show up in the tests. One of her daughters has allergies and her boyfriend has a drinking problem. Marilee also has a spastic colon, but who wouldn't with all the stress in her life?

Beth knows Marilee needs this job. She has told Marilee many times that she has to stop missing days and coming in late. And Beth did kind of put Marilee on probation (after getting a direct order to do it from Beth's boss, who doesn't have one ounce of compassion in her whole body). But Marilee just hasn't performed, and now Beth's boss has told her to fire her.

Beth thinks they ought to give Marilee another chance. She just knows that when Marilee gets her life together she'll be a real asset to the department. Everybody likes her, especially the customers. Beth thinks that her boss shouldn't be so hard nosed about this. Her boss points out that the rest of the department is complaining that Marilee gets special breaks.

Beth doesn't think it's fair. If her boss is so eager to show Marilee the door, the boss should fire Marilee herself!

Beth needs to fire her friend even though she is tempted to intercede with her boss to get Marilee another chance. Rules are rules, and Marilee has broken them repeatedly. Being kindhearted in this situation is hurting the other people in the department. Beth doesn't think it's fair that she should have to fire her friend. She may even be able to get her boss to do it for her if she asks.

If Beth lets her boss do the firing so that Beth can remain the "nice guy," her authority will be compromised with the rest of the department and Beth's boss will have some questions about her ability to do her job.

Beth really isn't helping Marilee by standing between her and the consequences of her actions. This, however, is an issue related to their friendship. Putting Marilee on probation and now firing her are part of Beth's job. The action that is most painful to Beth is really what is most advantageous to her and everyone else. (We will talk more about people like Marilee in the section on passive-aggressive behavior later in this chapter.)

Don't Let a Sacred Bull Be Your Lawyer

We are certainly not implying that there is no such thing as unfairness and discrimination in the workplace. However, suggesting that you are being asked to do things that others are not required to do, or that you are not being allowed to do what others may do, is a major accusation. It should be the last resort when negotiation fails, not the first thing out of your mouth.

If you have a question about what others are required or allowed to do, you need to check it out very carefully before you bring up the issue of possible discrimination with your boss. Even asking the question is a strong accusation.

The question, "Are other people required to do the same thing?" has become, unfortunately, a question for attorneys and courts to decide, certainly not for Sacred Bulls. If you think you are being discriminated against, check with a lawyer before you raise the issue. If you don't want to resort to tactical nuclear weapons, we recommend that you do your best to negotiate what *you* want or don't want to do and not worry about what other people are doing. We know this advice is not politically correct but it may save you a lot of trouble.

Know what you are talking about. Have evidence. Most important, don't mistake other fairness-related issues for discrimination. In many cases discrimination is a crime (and, in all cases, management will deny its existence). No doubt about it: Discrimination exists. However, if it is happening to you, you must be able to prove it, not just announce it and expect that someone else will look into it.

Most issues at work can be negotiated. However, if you bring up the topic of fairness itself, negotiation stops. You are then creating a barrier: good guys versus bad guys, a winner and a loser, right versus wrong. Believing that you can deal with office life in such simple, easy-to-understand terms will lead to disappointment and frustration—your own or that of the people around you. But it's what you get if you have a Sacred Bull for a lawyer.

"What? Me Angry?"

The major problem with fairness is that it is the concept that is easiest for aggression to hide behind. This Sacred Bull has a nasty sense of humor. It can turn people who see themselves as kind and giving into downright mean, demanding tyrants.

It's easier and less aggressive to say, "There are certain laws of the universe that are not being obeyed in this office," than to declare, "I want things my way or I'll take my marbles and go home!" If you appear to be fighting for fairness instead of your own interests, you can justify any number of abuses because they're for a noble cause.

Maybe you work with people who pursue fairness.

Their coworkers don't trust them and their bosses can't rely on them. All they know is that they haven't been treated fairly. Perhaps the most unpopular employees in any workplace are angry people who have made themselves victims of fairness. They usually are accused of having attitude problems or of not being team players. What they actually have in common is what psychologists call *passive-aggressive behavior*.

Maybe they've been passed over for promotion. Maybe others in their department are paid more. Maybe they think they work harder than the boss. If asked, however, they will deny that they're angry. They see themselves as fueled by moral outrage and a sense of injustice. (Especially obnoxious are employees who say, with a touch of noble sadness, "It's not myself I'm concerned about. It's others." Close behind are those who deny any interest in the specific issue but explain they are fighting for the "principle of the thing.")

Passive-aggressive people hide their aggression from themselves. They don't feel angry; they just do things that make others angry at them. Then they can feel justified in being angry at others for retaliating against them.

Other people don't know how to deal effectively with their behavior or even how to talk about it. But they know it when they see it.

A typical conversation with a passive-aggressive person goes:

"I know you're angry."
"No, I'm not."
"Yes, you are."
"No, I'm really not."

But get ready for a soliloquy if you ask, "Do you have any problems with your job?" or "Are you having problems working with someone?" They'll probably roll their eyes, sigh and say, "Well, I really shouldn't tell you this but. . . ." Then they'll talk for three hours straight if you let them, longer if you agree with them.

Passive-aggressive people believe they should not be angry. They have learned from childhood that anger is wrong. (Interesting that when people think something is wrong they often call it something else and do it anyway.) Passive-aggressive people are never angry, but they certainly can be holy terrors when they are "upset," "concerned," or even "confused." Even though they aren't angry, you often see them riding into battle, astride the Sacred Bull of Fairness.

At the end of the conversation they'll say, "Thanks so much. It feels good to get all this off my chest." What they've really been doing is justifying their own feelings of injustice and, with those feelings, their "right" to retaliate in the name of fairness. Their retaliation often involves forgetting to do whatever is most crucial to the boss's or the department's needs that day. (Forgetting is the passive-aggressive person's time-honored weapon.)

Passive-Aggressive Weapons: Annoy, Delay, and Sabotage

Passive-aggressive people seem to know how to choose the most effective tactic to annoy, delay, or sabotage. But try asking if they made the mistake on purpose. They will bristle and answer, "Absolutely not! How could you think such a thing? I've just been so overstressed lately that I can barely remember my own name. . . ."

Jordan says he's not the kind of person who gets angry easily. That may be true, but he doesn't seem to have any problem making people angry at him.

It's always a misunderstanding. When you ask Jordan to do something he doesn't want to do, he will either: (a) misunderstand and go ahead and do what he wanted to do

*in the first place, or (b) do nothing because he's sure you
misunderstood what you wanted him to do. (After all, you
didn't ask him to do it the way he wanted to.)*

*Jordan doesn't always act this way, of course. If he did
he would have been out on the street years ago. Most of the
time he's pretty good at what he's supposed to do. You just
never know when he's going to drop the ball. When he does,
his infractions are just below the level that could make him
eligible for formal discipline or firing.*

*He gets you every time. You always think, "I should
have known." Then the headache starts. You know Jordan
caused it as surely as if he'd conked you on the head with
a two-by-four. If you ask him about the problem—the
missed meeting, incomplete report, or botched job—he's
always the innocent victim of misunderstanding.*

Jordan deals with his anger in a passive-aggressive
way. To work with him effectively you have to know what
that means. First, he isn't lying. If you did what he's
doing, you'd have to lie to bring it off; Jordan doesn't. He
really doesn't know that he's angry and is fighting you
with his behavior. That is what passive-aggressive behavior is all about.

You will be frustrated if you try to get him to accept
that his behavior is intentional. People become passive-
aggressive because they cannot acknowledge their anger
at someone they care about, respect, or fear. (Such behavior occurs more often in personal relationships than
at work. It may be a small consolation, but Jordan's wife
probably has it harder than you do.)

The more Jordan likes, respects, or fears someone, the
less he is able to say directly, "I'm angry" or "I don't want
to do that." He has to rely on forgetting or misunderstanding to do the job for him.

Clear, explicit instructions are absolutely necessary in
dealing with someone like Jordan—but even clear directions will not work as well as you think they should.

In addition, structure short-term rewards and negative consequences so that he will gain more from doing things right and less from doing them wrong.

Most passive-aggressive people feel underappreciated. They need more praise than most people. Figure on offering Jordan about twice the amount of praise that would be appropriate for you (three times if you are particularly macho).

Chewing him out will definitely not work and will make the situation worse. He will just have more reason to fear you or to get back at you. Passive-aggressive people cause more trouble than they need to. Their dynamics are simple, and they respond well to praise and attention. What makes them so difficult is the natural tendency to get angry at their behavior. Publicly criticizing them or singling them out for punishment only makes more trouble for managers.

Whoever makes a mistake has to fix it. This simple policy (called *response cost*) will work well for passive-aggressive employees—as long as you also use it for everyone else. The idea for passive-aggressive people is to raise the price of their mistakes by making them do the kinds of work they dislike.

Paperwork often serves well as a response cost. Having Jordan fill out an "incident" report or mistake form may be effective. Or have him call or meet with the people who have to wait because of his mistake. If he suggests he is being punished, you can respond calmly, "It's just company policy. Whoever makes a mistake has to write it up or fix it." Let him know you'll be happy to discuss it *after* he does what you ask.

Passive-Aggressive Behavior Can Destroy a Career

Passive-aggressive people get fired, passed over, and discriminated against, and they don't have a clue that they are in part responsible. They see themselves as victims.

Erin prides herself on her fairness as a manager. She believes in "consensual management," which to her means that the team has to get together to make every decision. She wouldn't dare do anything without allowing everyone to have a say—unlike some other managers she knows. Erin firmly believes in her style. True, the meetings take up a lot of time but that's the price of fairness.

Erin's boss is always pressing her to come up with decisions, but she will not act without clearing it with her team. She thinks this is the secret of high morale, and she subtly communicates her belief that her department is the only oasis of caring in a desert of unconcern.

Actually, Erin's team has the lowest morale in the entire division. Her department has divided into two distinct camps. One group thinks she is the greatest manager in the world and that she and her team are completely undervalued by the rest of the organization.

The other half sees Erin as unable to make a decision. They resent having to spend hours and hours in meetings. On most issues, they wish Erin would just make the call and give them the extra time to do their work. They say this at nearly every meeting, but Erin points out that somebody has an opinion on everything, and everybody must be heard.

Erin thinks she is democratic and fair. She actually is ramming her style down the unwilling throats of people who have no need for a say on everything. She doesn't like to be pushed, so she pushes people into not being pushed. This kind of logic is typical with passive-aggressive people.

Erin's management style is a passive-aggressive reaction to the authoritarian styles she sees around her. Everyone suffers—Erin most of all. Nobody in her department is happy. They just differ in what they're unhappy about. Some are peeved at the rest of the company for not being like Erin. Some are irritated by Erin.

Erin believes that it is almost criminally unfair to expect people to work when they're sick. She wouldn't think of coming in when her colitis is acting up. She will often send people home if they cough, sniffle, or have a headache. Consequently, Erin's department has the lowest productivity and highest absentee rate in the division. Upper management's continual pressure about this only underscores to Erin how unfair and exploitive this company is.

Finally Erin decided to resign—and it took her an unfairly long time to find another job. She had a number of interviews and was even offered one job. Then the offer was retracted because she couldn't negotiate an acceptable contract of employment with the company. When Erin's terms reached ten pages, they said, "Maybe you're in the wrong place."

Erin doesn't see that her belief in fairness is really her way of fighting back against the people she expects will try to take advantage of her with their high-handed, authoritarian behavior. Erin has no idea that she has an authority problem. She thinks she's the fairest in the land.

Erin does not realize that she appears angry to others. She says she wants only to be treated fairly—the way she treats others! (Or the way she thinks she treats others. Others treat Erin with the same distrust and dislike that she communicates.)

Erin will become more bitter until she recognizes that her expectations of fairness are creating just the situations she hopes to avoid. (Erin and her team will continue to feel angry and unappreciated. Her colitis will get worse; she may find a way out through disability.)

DON'T BECOME A MISGUIDED MISSILE

Passive-aggressive people can get you to do their fighting for them. By communicating to you that they are being taken advantage of and are helpless to do anything about it, they can send you speeding toward their target like a misguided missile.

You've seen Karen many times, squinting at her display and pounding away at her keyboard as you were leaving to go home. She's a hard worker, but you know she doesn't really want to be working all these extra hours. Karen can't say no, and Doug, her boss, continually takes advantage of her. He gives her huge reports and projects that have to be ready the next day "or else" (or else Doug's rear will be in a sling).

You've worked with Doug for awhile and think he's insensitive and unfair. You're worried that Karen might quit, which would be terrible. The whole department depends on her skills. She's a pillar of the organization and a wonderful person, which is more than you can say for Doug.

You want to help, so you take Karen aside for a little friendly advice. You tell her the only way Doug will ever change is if she tells him no. You even loan her the assertiveness book you read back in 1982. Karen thanks you effusively, smiles, and nods.

A few weeks later Karen's still working late. She hasn't taken your advice. She hasn't read the book (she's been too busy). She confides that her back is acting up and her doctor has advised her to take some time off, which, of course, she can't do.

You say firmly, "Karen, you've just got to talk with Doug!" She smiles sadly and nods, and you know she won't do it.

So you do it. You tell Doug what's going on. You're respectful and polite and make it clear that you are just trying to be helpful. After all, fair is fair.

Doug does not take your comments in the spirit intended. In fact, he gets irritated. "Karen never told me this," he says (as if you made it up). "Okay, I'll talk to her about it."

Doug talks to Karen, who says the long hours aren't really so bad. She does add that her husband is getting upset and her backaches are getting worse (which is as close to no as she can come). Insensitive clod that he is, Doug does not see that this has anything to do with him or with what he's talking about.

Next time you see Doug he tells you that he's talked to Karen and everything's taken care of. The next night you see her working late again. You ask her what happened and all you get is a flood of tears.

You didn't mean for things to turn out this way. You were only trying to help, but now Karen's situation seems worse than before and you're feeling responsible (and very ticked off at Doug).

What to do now?

That's easy, you think. You'll do what any decent person would do. You charge down the hall, riding the Bull of Fairness, toward the office of Doug's boss, feeling like a hero. You are battling not for yourself but for Karen and, yes, for justice!

Before the day is out, however, you'll be treated like a villain. You're so intent on helping Karen that you may not realize that you're playing havoc with the chain of command as well as being a tattletale, both of which are bigger corporate sins than exploiting an employee. You also may not see that Karen has set you up with her helplessness.

This scenario can end in many ways, none of which will be good for you or Karen. If Doug's boss is naive enough to intervene and reprimand Doug, both you and Karen will end up on Doug's short list. Much more likely, however, is that Doug's boss will listen to you, do nothing, and secretly lower her opinion of you.

When people can't speak up for themselves, you harm everyone by speaking for them, even if this seems like the fair and charitable thing to do.

In this situation:

- You harm Karen by taking away whatever motivation she had to speak up for herself. You have done it for her (as she hoped you would).
- You harm the organization by abandoning direct communication and meddling in someone's else's business.
- You harm your own reputation.

The only person you don't hurt is Doug, the person who is most to blame. He emerges as the injured party, and his mistreatment of Karen takes a backseat to your meddling.

What should you do when your colleague is a victim of unfair treatment?

Talk to Karen. Encourage her. Loan her the assertiveness book. Even rehearse the scene with her. But if she doesn't speak for herself, don't try to rescue her. You can keep trying to motivate her but don't speak up for her. If you become her misguided missile, you blow up everything except the target you wanted to hit.

How to Be Seen as a Fair Leader

Fairness is a damaging concept only when you're thinking about other people being fair to *you*. When, however, you think of fairness in terms of how other people would like you to treat *them*, then fairness can make your life a lot easier and more productive.

If you're a manager, chances are that you have been accused of being unfair, whether you have been or not.

Part of the problem comes with the management territory and has nothing to do with fairness.

If you are in charge, everything you do will be magnified by your subordinates. If you correct someone, it's a tongue-lashing. If you forget something, you have Alzheimer's. If you make a mistake, you're incompetent. Your power makes everything seem bigger. Also, everyone, no matter how grown up, has a "teenager" inside who resents being told what to do and looks for evidence that any authority figure abuses power.

Being perceived as a fair leader is good business. People are much more likely to be loyal to and to do a good job for a boss whom they perceive as fair. They will work harder and take more responsibility if they think they're in a situation that's fair. They will see the organization as fair when what's best for the company takes precedence over the personal desires of the people with power.

The odds are daunting, but being perceived as fair by your employees is worth the effort. The secret is showing that you see things from their point of view and can understand how they might decide whether you were fair or unfair. They will base their perception of fairness less on what you say and more on what you do day to day, or on what you appear to do if they don't know what you actually do.

1. *Roll up your sleeves and work alongside your employees as often as possible.*   Or let them know what you do when you're not directly visible. If you spend a lot of time at meetings, tell people about the meeting topics that affect them and what you did for your department. Educate them about what you do.

2. *Be specific.*   Clearly specify what it takes to do a good job. Let people know when they get it right at least as often as you tell them when they get it wrong.

3. *Don't ask people to do things that are not their responsibility.*   Of course there is room for discussion on this

issue, and this discussion should occur, particularly
when there is disagreement. You need to explain why the
requested task is the employee's responsibility. You do
not always need to follow a rigid job description but you
do need to stop asking employees to do things that make
them look and feel like personal servants. Asking someone to pick up your dry cleaning or to make your coffee,
for example, will earn you negative PR and heighten the
perception that you are an unfair boss.

4. *Don't make employees do things that hurt, demean,
or get them in trouble.* If you plan to make such an
assignment, warn employees of the risk beforehand.

5. *Recognize that punishment is the easiest—but least
effective—form of behavior control.* Avoid the temptation to chew people out. Believe us, it costs more than
it's worth. Set contingencies and stick to them. When
something goes wrong, fix the problem rather than trying
to fix the blame.

6. *See that rewards and punishments are predictably
based on what you say.* If there are rules, follow them
or change them. Nothing erodes the perception of fairness as much as having rules on the books that are en-
forced only when convenient.

7. *Be visibly evenhanded.* In theory, fairness means
that the same standards apply to everyone. This is difficult to do and even more difficult to see, because everyone's perception of fairness begins with wondering if
other people are getting better breaks. As a manager you
not only have to be fair, you also have to step in and
speak up for evenhandedness.

It is easier to give the most important work to the best
workers and to assign less-crucial tasks to people who
are not quite up to speed. The result, however, is that
your best employees may end up feeling that you are
"rewarding" them with more work and letting the goof-
offs slip by. Training the less-efficient employees or de-

manding more from them takes more time and effort but will earn you points with the hard workers.

8. *Fire people rather than forcing them to resign.* (Your corporate attorney will probably disagree with this advice. The truth is that nothing erodes morale more than having an employee around who is slowly being driven out.)

9. *Remember the first rule of PR.* To be considered a fair leader, remember the first rule of public relations: "What it looks like is more important than what it is." If your employees see you as fair, they will do nearly anything for you. If they don't, they will do what is required and nothing more.

On a corporate level, fairness, or being perceived as fair, is good business because it instills loyalty. In a workplace in which punishment is the main source of control, people will tend to retaliate or simply not do all the positive things they could be doing. The less they do, the less likely they are to get punished; this is a normal and predictable response to management by punishment. The result, of course, is that people will stop being self-starters and empowered employees.

THE BULL OF EXCUSES
There's a Good Reason!

T*he quarterly meeting has come to order. Departmental performance has not been dazzling this quarter, to say the least. The competition is muscling into our market share, sales are sliding, and costs are edging up out of control. Morale is at an all-time low. Requests for transfers are piling up like dead leaves under a ficus tree.*

Beaming as usual, Cliff, the department head, steps up to the plate. His smile seems reassuring to the two VPs from headquarters, as they look up from the handouts they have been thumbing through. They want some good news to take back with them. You can see it in their eyes and in the bullets of sweat forming on their brows.

Everything depends on how well Cliff can put a positive spin on what's been happening around here.

"Sales are slow," he begins heartily, "but in a way that is a good sign. Our economists tell us that people are uncertain which way the economy is moving so they are adopting a wait-and-see attitude. They are still considering purchases, but they are not ready to part with their money just yet.

"Marketing tells us that the name recognition and approval ratings for our products are higher than at this time last year—much higher. Added together they show a 15 percent increase."

Cliff continues quickly, giving no one time to realize he has just blatantly doubled the number by adding two statistics that measure different things. "What we are talking about, ladies and gentlemen, is a classic 'pent-up demand' situation."

His voice rises with high drama. "People want our products, but they are not buying them until they feel sure of the economic situation." His smile reflects sympathy for all the yearning customers. "The good news is that the economy is picking up, as you can see from the forecasts my assistants are handing out now. We should be seeing some benefits from this pent-up demand by spring perhaps, summer at the latest."

Cliff's words ring with assurance. "An increase equal to the amount of improvement in the marketing survey—15 percent—would not be out of the question. Between now and then we are moving into position with a strategic right-sizing program. By spring we ought to be ready and organized to cash in on the positive turn in the economy!"

The VPs are smiling like pacified toddlers.

As Cliff continues with his presentation, you marvel at his adeptness. What this guy does is amazing. He's making spin-doctoring history. You would have said, "Customers aren't buying our stuff and we don't know why; furthermore, people in the department are quitting and transferring out."

NOTHING A LITTLE SPIN-DOCTORING WON'T CURE

All too often things don't turn out the way we expect or want them to. Most of us have a whole set of mental and verbal behaviors ready to use almost automatically when things go wrong. We make excuses. We justify our actions. We explain why things didn't happen according to plan. Spin-doctoring, a practice all too common in business and politics, is the elevation of an excuse to an art form.

The theory behind making excuses is that if you knew why something went wrong you would know what to do to make it right. However, between theory and practice falls a dark, horned shadow. (No, not him. The Devil may be in the details but the Bull is in the excuses.)

This Sacred Bull will try to convince you that a good excuse is the moral equivalent of a good action. Stated this way, of course, the idea sounds ludicrous, but the problem is that it never is stated this way. The Bull of Excuses is a silver-tongued devil. That's his job.

Excuses do damage both to the people who make them and to the people who believe them. Most of us expect excuses. We hear them and make them so often that we seldom think about what we're hearing or what we're doing. Excuses are reasons we all give to explain why we should not have to face the consequences of our behavior—at least, this time.

Usually the excuses are almost automatic. They offer propositions that make little sense if we look at them closely. A close examination, however, is the best defense against this Sacred Bull. To protect ourselves from the dangers of making and believing excuses, we need to look more closely at what excuses are and why they work.

WHY EXCUSES WORK

Effective excuses deliver people from the consequences of their behaviors. All good excuses offer something that is enough more positive than actual reality so that people will want to believe them. This is why excuses such as

"The dog ate my homework" seldom work even when they're true. They only explain what happened and offer no incentive for believing them. A good excuse must offer people what they want to believe.

While we pass excuses back and forth like hard currency, most of us rarely stop to consider why some kinds of excuses are more effective than others. It is essential to know this, even if you have no intention of deceiving other people. You need to know how excuses work. You need to realize that a good enough excuse may deceive you. You may even use one to deceive yourself.

Tension Reduction

Good excuses always relieve tension. When people are tense they are much more apt to dole out negative consequences. They are more apt to yell at us, fire us, or take their business elsewhere. One of the most common sources of people's tension is discovering that what they want is not ready when they want it. This is where the old "It'll be ready soon" ploy comes in—a way to prevent the consequences of being late.

"The report isn't ready. I know you are expecting it for the meeting tomorrow morning, but we're waiting for two more sets of figures from the branch offices. They'll be in by this afternoon. I know because I called the branch office and they said they're almost done. They'll fax them to me as soon as they're ready. The minute I get the figures, I'll put the report together. I'll work late. It will be on your desk when you come in tomorrow morning."

Either the report will be there or you'll find a note explaining why it isn't there. (But that's another story.) Excuses like this work because they relieve tension.

You need the report, you don't have it, you start feeling tense. You accept the excuse because it calms you down.

The excuse is effective not only because you believe the report will be there tomorrow but also because it gives you an alternative to taking unpleasant action in the form of imposing consequences. (What are you going to do when a subordinate says the report is not ready—fire him? You still need the report.) Other than the report itself, the most positive alternative you could get is the belief that it will be here soon and that your subordinate considers it just as important as you do. Your tension is relieved because there is less you have to do.

(Yes, we know you're the kind of manager who will stay on the case and make sure the figures are in and the report arrives on time. The excuse would still relieve some tension because at least you know your subordinates are taking this seriously. If you are particularly compulsive, you might require extra tension relief. You might want to get on the phone to the branch offices and hear their excuses firsthand. That will make you feel better.)

Everybody Wins

To work well, an excuse has to lower the tension for both people—the one making the excuse and the one hearing it—by preventing negative consequences for both. The employee doesn't get fired, and the boss doesn't have to stay up all night doing the report.

A good excuse is the quintessential win/win proposition. It transfers all the negative possibilities from right now to some indefinite point in the future. The excuse sounds good. No wonder the temptation is strong to believe it, even when we know better.

SPIN-DOCTORING: RAISING EXCUSES TO AN ART FORM

The ultimate in effective excuses is spin-doctoring. This involves taking a very negative turn of events and presenting it as only slightly less positive than whatever you had actually wanted to happen. Needless to say, this requires considerable verbal deftness and knowledge of what your audience wants to hear. (That's why it takes a doctorate to do it.)

One of the most effective spin-doctor tactics in business is to declare, "We were doing the right things; it's just the results that came out wrong." If excuses are well crafted enough, they can be accepted as almost equivalent to positive results—even by the people who craft them. If that's not a fertile pasture for Bulls, we don't know what is.

Remember Cliff, the master spin-doctor, at the beginning of the chapter? He presented low sales (with some artificially inflated marketing statistics) as an indication of pent-up demand that would miraculously turn itself into a burst of sales as soon as the economy picked up. This is spin-doctoring at its finest. It prevents all kinds of negative consequences.

As "Dr." Cliff spun onward for the VPs, his private thoughts were spinning in a different direction: This is a lot better than admitting that our product isn't selling and we really don't know why. We can't allow ourselves to say that. It would sound, well, stupid. Instead, I'm giving these stiffs some smart-sounding reasons that make our ignorance and mistakes a little harder to see.

As you have seen in previous chapters, ignorance and mistakes are worse lapses in many business settings than lack of results. This is one reason why spin-doctoring is in such demand.

Cliff winds up with a confident grin. "All we have to do is wait until next quarter and hope the economy picks up so that pent-up demand will be busting the lid off our sales quotas!"

The other negative consequence that Cliff's spin-doctoring helps avoid is having to do anything about the problem. It's a neat trick.

Of course, if you had been one of Cliff's VPs, we know you would be very skeptical about a sales report like the one Cliff just presented—mainly because it wasn't prepared for *you*. Spin-doctoring requires precise knowledge about exactly what a person wants to believe. When it's done right, it makes you an offer that you *personally* can't refuse.

Spin-doctoring is a real skill. You have to admit that there's a certain perverse beauty to it as well as a good deal of hidden danger. Luckily there are few people who will spend the time and effort to find out what you want to believe enough to do a really expert job of spin-doctoring you.

The biggest danger always comes from an excuse made up by someone who already knows what you want. Consequently the most effective and dangerous spin-doctor for you is *yourself*. We will consider this more fully later in the chapter. First, we have to look more closely at the problem with excuses.

The Problem with Excuses

Although the Bull of Excuses may shield us from punishment and ridicule, the Bull also shields us from learning.

It is the consequences of our behaviors that we learn from. If the Bull had his way, we would all remain in a state of blameless ignorance. The irony is that we could see through most excuses if we looked. Most of us choose not to look. If we did, we might see things we don't want to see.

Rachel can hardly believe it. It's five minutes to nine and the meeting might actually happen. For the last three weeks Nguyen had canceled their regular supervisory session. Rachel was beginning to think she was so low on his priority list that she'd finally dropped off the page completely.

She's ready for today. She has about a million things to discuss, all laid out neatly in her planner. She has prioritized and even budgeted time for each issue so she can make the best use of this hour.

Just as she's getting her material together, the phone rings. Nguyen is on the line. "Rachel, you won't believe this. I'm stuck upstairs in one of those endless planning meetings. It looks like it's going to go way over schedule. You know how the old man likes to talk."

Before Rachel can respond, her boss continues. "I'm really sorry. Look, this week is really hectic for me. Why don't we just make it next week at this same time, okay? I really hate to do this to you, but you know how crazy things are around here. My time is just not my own."

Rachel swallows her frustration and says, "Okay, Nguyen. I understand. But let's make sure we get together next week. I have a lot of issues that really need your input."

"Absolutely. Of course. Next week for sure. It's my top priority," her boss says as he hangs up.

If you were Rachel, would you believe that you were top priority? Rachel would like to believe that meeting with her is important to her boss and that missing meetings doesn't really mean that she is not worth his time.

She would like to believe that what he says means more than what he does.

This is what gives the Bull of Excuses much of his power to deceive. Excuses can offer a more palatable version of reality than what is available from the other evidence. We want to believe what we hear, so we do—even when, at some level, we know we're being hoodwinked.

Nguyen is attempting a balancing act. He doesn't have time to do everything, and Rachel is a lower priority than some of the other things he has going. His excuse is an attempt to soften the blow for Rachel and perhaps to convince himself as well. His excuse prevents him from having to ask himself why he is avoiding Rachel. Is she just unimportant or are there problems in their working relationship?

Excuses make everything simpler in the short run. Over the long run Nguyen's excuses create problems. He is sending Rachel a double message: You are important but not important enough for me to keep my appointments with you. By attempting to avoid hurting her feelings, he is risking losing her trust.

Nguyen is coming up with excuses automatically on the spur of the moment. He doesn't want to hurt Rachel's feelings, and she doesn't want to be hurt. So the excuse passes. It is only after this scenario plays out a few times that Rachel (and other people whose feelings Nguyen has tried to avoid hurting) will begin to wonder how much of what he says they can believe.

EVENTUALLY EXCUSES CATCH UP WITH US

Excuses are like Julius Caesar. The evil they do lives after them and the good is often interred with their bones. Their main purpose is to defer the consequences of behavior from the present to the future. The problem is

that our best source of learning is the immediate consequences of our acts.

*Okay, okay, Wayne knows his goals haven't quite been
met this quarter. There's a lot of turnover in the whole
division and, as everybody knows, there have been some
foul-ups with orders reaching his department in the first
place. He's not mentioning any names, but the problems
are a matter of record.*

*Don't forget that right in the middle of the quarter several
of the models changed abruptly and customers had to be
educated. Also, we're looking at the period that was on the
tail end of the shift to the new inventory system.*

Wayne can go on for hours.

*All right, you decide, you'll give him the benefit of the
doubt.*

What will Wayne learn from that?

One thing he'll learn is that a good excuse (or a long
string of them) is as acceptable as good results. This will
obviously hurt the company. You can't pay dividends on
excuses. Unless the company is very loosely managed,
the damage will be short run. Eventually his excuses will
catch up with him.

If Wayne is using excuses instead of results, eventually
someone will notice and demand he be put on probation
until his performance improves. Who finally notices and
how long it takes to figure it out will determine how
many other people go down with Wayne. Unless he is an
extremely silver-tongued spin-doctor, however, Wayne
will eventually take the fall—even though he has been
taught that excuses will protect him.

In many workplaces the consequences seem to teach
us that excuses are okay. This is incorrect. The truth is
that most employees are allowed a certain number of
excuses. When they use those up, it's good-bye Charlie
(or Wayne).

Every excuse, even if it's true, puts a strain on your credibility. You don't know when your credibility will break. When it does, you lose something—most often your freedom. Your boss or coworkers will have to check up on you. People will accept your excuses in a polite and friendly way until they get fed up and refuse to listen anymore. Then they clamp down.

The more you rely on excuses (if you're adept at all), the more you learn they work. They relieve tension. They buy you time. They keep people liking you. Until it's too late, you don't learn about the abrupt end of tolerance. Excuses do you damage, but the damage is somewhere down the line.

The big trouble doesn't come until long after you've had a chance to get very good at making excuses. You may be tempted to explain to yourself that the person who clamps down, gets angry, or demands proof is merely out of sorts. It is quite easy to spin-doctor the situation so it looks to you as if the problem lies with the other person, not with you. The only person who doesn't seem to get fed up with your excuses is yourself.

The price you pay in the end is even higher than messing up and getting chewed out. The cost of excuses is the perception of your own control over your life. As you saw in chapter 6 on blame (one of the most common kinds of excuses), trying to escape consequences can get you into the far more dangerous trap of believing you have no control over what happens to you.

SPIN-DOCTORING YOURSELF

Using excuses on other people is damaging, but even more destructive is the damage you can do when you try to spin-doctor yourself. It's not hard to become your own spin-doctor. You know best what you want to believe.

When you start believing your own excuses, you can open the door to troublesome and destructive behaviors and never even see them come in. The Bull of Excuses works best in the dark.

The less attention you pay to the excuses you give yourself, the more likely they are to just slip by and become a part of your reality before you even know what's happening. Although the Bull of Excuses prefers the dark, he can come up with a million justifications why the rules shouldn't apply even if you turn on the lights.

"I Work So Hard, I Deserve a Break"

A common justification is, "I work so hard, I deserve a break." This is a little-known loophole in the work ethic that says hard work exempts you from other responsibilities. (If you want to know what others think of this reasoning, just ask the families of people who regularly put in sixty-hour weeks and say, "I work hard to bring in the money to give you the kind of life you want. How dare you demand that I be available to spend time with you?" Their families might want to make do with less money and more time, but they don't get the choice.)

"I'll Do It In a Few Minutes"

This excuse—"I'll do it in a few minutes"—serves to cover the distance between intentions and actions. You know what you need to do. It is important that you do it. Of course, you *will* do it, just as soon as you take care of the things you absolutely have to do first. You can recycle the excuse until the few minutes stretch into hours, then days. Eventually you realize that you are just too busy to do it at all.

"I Was Too Busy"

Perhaps the most destructive justification is the simplest: "I was too busy." If we don't pay close enough attention to what we're saying, we can justify doing things that are not consistent with our values.

The report from the safety committee is on Jake's desk. He has glanced at it and has seen a list of recommendations. Some of them are typical petty things like moving the fire extinguisher six feet to the right. But there is some significant stuff, too. Jake knows some of the equipment is old and isn't working as well as it should. It probably should be replaced but that takes money and time, and this section of the company is barely keeping its head above water as it is.

Jake is committed to his employees. He does not believe in subjecting them to undue hazards on the job, but there are so many other things going on and this safety report is such a thorny issue. So the report sits on Jake's desk. He's not burying it; it's burying itself, actually.

Jake is concerned with safety, but he can justify not doing anything about it because he is just too busy to get to it. Jake is spin-doctoring himself. He wants to believe that safety is a high priority with him, even if he doesn't commit time and resources to it. He judges himself by what is in his heart rather than by what he does. It makes sense, if he doesn't look at it too closely.

This is something we all do. Our larger priorities somehow submerge in the deluge of day-to-day tasks. The problem comes when we spin-doctor ourselves. Instead of saying, "My priorities have shifted; I'd better do something about it," we say, "My priorities are the same as they always were. It's just that I'm too busy to live by them at the moment."

Of course, we would never believe this from someone

else, but we want so much to believe it of ourselves that we do. All of us believe in spending quality time with our families, planning for the future, and doing things for those less fortunate than ourselves. Most of us are too busy to do as much of these things as we believe we should. Nevertheless, we still see them as top priorities in our lives. Actions seldom speak louder than the Bull of Excuses.

When we believe our own excuses, we are saying to ourselves, "I should be held responsible only for the consequences of my intentions rather than the consequences of my actions." We can really believe that the rules that apply to other people do not apply to us if our intentions are good.

The road to Hell, they say, is paved with good intentions. It is the Bull of Excuses who holds the paving contract. We say to ourselves, "I don't have to follow this particular rule because I'm following other rules that are more important." We say this long and loudly, so loudly that we don't have to think about the rules we aren't following.

WHEN THE BULL BLOCKS YOUR VIEW

These justifications come up mostly after the fact, when you have to explain what you have done to yourself. Most of the time you're never called upon to explain. The Bull of Excuses can make you too busy or distracted to think of the impact your actions (or inaction) might have on other people.

We all go through this process. It's part of being human. The process itself is not evil, but it is the door we must all pass through to do things that are inconsistent with our values. How much light there is around this door, how wide it opens and, most of all, when it closes are the elements of what is commonly called conscience.

The main job of the Bull of Excuses is to block your view so you can't see the door at all while the Bull says reassuringly, "Just keep moving."

Cody doesn't believe in stealing, but you might not be convinced of that by looking closely at his tax return. He calls it creative accounting. Most of the time he just does it; he doesn't think about why he does it. When he asks himself, he justifies the cheating because he's darn sure the IRS is trying to steal from him. Besides, it's a well-known fact that the big guys with their fancy tax lawyers get all these loopholes so they don't have to pay any taxes at all. A little guy like Cody needs to invent his own loopholes.

Anyway, the government wastes so much money that the little bit Cody reappropriates wouldn't make any difference to anybody. One less ashtray for the Pentagon maybe. Besides, saving a few dollars on your taxes isn't stealing, is it? It's not like breaking into somebody's house and taking something that doesn't belong to you. Right?

Cody buries the fundamental issue in a flurry of excuses. Is cheating on your taxes the same as stealing? The law says so. Cody could say, "I'm breaking the law, and if I'm caught I'll face the consequences." Instead, he works things around in his mind so that the law doesn't really apply and his obligation to himself takes precedence over his obligation to society.

He would never approve of that conclusion drawn by anyone else. Cody's a decent guy. He stands for law and order. It's just that some laws are more important than others. The ones that apply to others are more important than the ones that apply to him.

It is through this process that decent people can spin-doctor themselves into doing things they don't approve of. They can convince themselves that they're not really doing them because they don't *intend* to do them. It is not up to us to lecture our readers on morality. Morality is personal and private. Sacred Bulls, however, can creep even into the places closest to your heart. Unless you understand how they operate, they can do more damage than you ever intended.

Excuses That Don't Always Work

Effective excuses do damage to the people who make them as well as to the people who believe them. Ineffective excuses merely blow up in the faces of their creators. They make the people who hear them angrier at the excuse than at whatever the person making the excuse did in the first place.

"I Didn't Mean To"

This kind of excuse creeps into the business world from personal life, where it is generally more effective. If people care what you think of them, they may buy an excuse that sells them the proposition that even though you did the wrong thing, your intent was not to hurt or anger them.

"What's the idea of sending this memo without checking with me first?" Red-faced with anger, Reg waved the offending document under Sally's nose. "These changes in procedure affect my department directly. We agreed you would clear this kind of thing with me before you send it out."

Sally stopped herself from rolling her eyes. What's the big deal here? she silently wondered. It only changes two lines in a form they have to fill out. She recognized, however, that she had stepped on Reg's very sensitive toes—again.

Sally sighed. "Reg, I didn't mean to upset you. I thought it wasn't a big enough issue that it would concern you."

Reg's face turned crimson. "That's the point I'm making. You need to check with me first because you don't know! How can you say you didn't mean to upset me when we've discussed this issue many times and agreed that any procedural changes that affect my department need to be discussed with me first?"

Reg was just getting warmed up.

Sally would have done far better just to admit she had made a mistake and apologize. In the heat of the moment, however, she pulled a strategy out of the air that relieved more tension for her than for Reg. The situation escalated, and it will continue to escalate until she offers an abject apology.

Saying "I didn't mean to" may be a good approach with an indulgent spouse, but with coworkers or bosses it is considerably more risky. Knowing you weren't actually trying to tick them off may be much less important to them than your failing to take the actions they were expecting.

"I Forgot" and "I Was Too Busy"

Daryl's voice vibrated with irritation. "Why didn't you call me back? I needed to talk to you before we finished up with the contracts. I left you two messages."

Kathy's stomach turned over. "Oh, Daryl, I'm so sorry! I had the phone messages clipped to my appointment book. I meant to call you, but things got so hectic that I just forgot until I got home last night. By then it was too late."

"I forgot" and "I was too busy" are the most commonly used excuses, probably because they feel like the truest explanation of events. We do get busy and forget. As a strategy, however, these excuses carry a usually unintended risk. The other person may interpret what you're saying as "What I was supposed to do for you was less important than the other things I had to do."

Daryl shook his head and sighed. "Kathy, I don't know what you could have been doing that was more important than getting the contracts out. I had to spend an hour on the phone with the people in Chicago, assuring them we'd make the deadline."

The I-was-too-busy excuse works best when you can slip it by on people who are equally busy and forgetful. This is why it is also the most common excuse people use on themselves.

Kathy was glad Daryl didn't know she had spent most of the afternoon on the phone with the contractor for the house she is building. She would agree in a second that getting back to Daryl so that the contracts could go out was a much higher priority—but the house was on her mind and . . .

Like most people, Kathy got distracted from what was important to what was immediate. Her automatic excuse blocked her from considering the need to change her own actions. She spin-doctored herself as she made her excuses to Daryl. Most of us are not accustomed to considering the implications of our own excuses. No wonder this Bull is so powerful.

Excuses That Never Work

The kind of excuse that never works is the one that lowers tension for the person making the excuse by raising tension for the person hearing the excuse. The common name for this kind of excuse is *getting defensive*. Defensive excuses can be spectacularly ineffective and destructive. A few of the most widely used include:

"It was your fault anyway."
"You didn't give me the right information."
"What you did was worse!"
"You're always picking on me."

It is easy to see why these excuses would never work. Each depends for its effectiveness on the other person saying, "Oh, I get it. You were right and I was wrong. Sorry for the inconvenience." Nevertheless, people try to use them because they feel as if they ought to be true. When we use these excuses, we fervently hope the other person will believe them as much as we do.

A slightly less futile version is trying to shift the blame onto some unsuspecting third party. As we said in chapter 6 on blame, this strategy is also loaded with hidden problems, but it may get you off the hook for a short time.

Explanations Turn into Excuses

"I wasn't making an excuse! I was only *explaining*!" How many times have you heard someone say that? When people explain, it usually means they're explaining that if something went wrong, it wasn't their fault. In other words, they're making an excuse.

An excuse is a way to hide the consequences of your own behavior. An explanation can be a way to accept responsibility and move on toward resolving the problem. Unfortunately, it can also be a way to sneak an excuse by without taking responsibility for it.

"It's the Computer's Fault"

When something goes wrong, we are usually asked for an explanation. When we explain what happened from our own point of view, what we say tends to drift into the kind of excuse that relieves tension for ourselves but not for the person listening to our excuse. This kind of excuse makes people angry. We don't mean to do this. It just happens as a natural result of the way we see reality.

An irate customer calls. Only part of what he has ordered has been shipped, and he wants to know where the rest of the order is. He is being extremely colorful and rude about expressing his displeasure.

You call up his order on your screen, which shows exactly what was shipped. There is no record of the other products he says he ordered. What are you to think? It looks to you as if he forgot to order everything he wanted.

But what would happen if you tried to explain reality as you see it by saying to your customer, "I don't see it here on the screen. Are you sure you ordered it?"

This is barely an explanation, just a reasonable question based on what you see in front of you. But it is already shaping up into the kind of excuse that makes *you* feel good and your customer see red. (It is a well-known fact that 99.8 percent of all errors in business orders are made by two culprits: the computer or "the new girl" (or guy). But no customer will ever thank you for explaining that.) An explanation like this will just make your customer angrier and more likely to pick on you, even though you were clearly explaining that it wasn't your fault.

Try it this way if you want to see why the explanation doesn't work: "I'm willing to help, but first I want you to acknowledge that if anything goes wrong here, it certainly wasn't my fault."

That is the message the customer hears. To him, it is merely irrelevant and insulting information. It has nothing to do with getting him what he wants or relieving his tension.

In the reality you see and believe in, you are always doing what you're supposed to be doing. If you make an occasional mistake, there are always very good reasons for it. Other people see the world in much the same way, except that they are the center of it. So if there is a mistake and you explain what is so clear and obvious to you—that it wasn't your fault—there may be a big conflict with reality as the other person sees it (especially if there's no computer or new guy to blame).

"You Never Told Me"

When things go wrong, most explanations you might give on the spot come out sounding like, "So you see, I can't possibly be wrong, so you must be." This is a blatant contradiction of reality as the other person sees it.

The report is in and on time. You worked hard on it. The details are polished and the narrative flows. You put it on your boss's desk with great pride, expecting that she'll be impressed. An hour later, she calls you in. You enter smiling, expecting at least a "good work!"

Instead she says, "Where are the analyses for the last five years?" In your heart, you know she never asked for them. You're feeling unfairly accused, and an explanation is ready to burst from your lips. You want to say, "You never told me you wanted that!" Should you say it?

If you say it, there will be an argument. Even though what you're stating is to you merely a fact, your boss will take it as an accusation. This is a difficult situation. How can you be true to yourself and avoid telling your boss that she was the one who blew it? Even the most adept spin-doctoring will sound like what it is: spin-doctoring. What do you do?

One way to handle a situation like this is to shift from talking about what already happened (or didn't happen) to what is going on right now. When you do, focus on the other person's reality first, rather than your own:

"Anne, I know you're disappointed. I know you need that report and you need it to be right. What I gave you was not what you wanted. I hope you know that never in a million years would I do that intentionally. Your opinion of my work is very important to me, and I certainly don't want to blow it over this report. My intention was to give you what you needed. That is still my intention. What do we need to do?"

The only way Anne will be convinced that she never told you is if she comes to that conclusion herself. Your best bet is to remind her of how conscientious you are and leave it at that.

The issue is not who was right about the specifics of the report, but Anne's opinion of you as an employee. That is what you want to preserve. You can't possibly do that by saying, "Anne, the fact is you were the one who blew it, not me." Maybe later you can discuss it with less emotional involvement, but right now Anne is upset because she doesn't have what she needs. It is her tension that you need to lower. You need to acknowledge that as the most important issue here, rather than your own need for vindication.

Shifting to what is going on now and focusing on the other person's needs is the best way to thwart the Bull of Excuses. The purpose of excuses is to delay the consequences of your actions, even if you are not aware of your purpose because you are "only explaining." This is almost never in your best interest because there is a real chance that your excuse will make the other person angrier than what you did or didn't do. Also, the consequences of your action are the most effective tools for learning.

A Substitute for Excuses

If you're going to offer an excuse, try to find one that lowers tensions for both of you. If you're not that devious, we suggest a golden oldie:

"I made a mistake. I'm sorry. What can I do to correct it?" ("Here's what I'm willing to do to correct it" is also acceptable.)

This response may not feel correct. We almost always believe we're right and the other guy is wrong. And this response isn't really an excuse, because it doesn't defer any consequences. It does, however, beat the heck out of the troubles even effective excuses can make for you in the long run.

When Explanations Are Valuable

Of course there are times when things don't go as planned and need to be analyzed and explained so you won't make the same mistakes again. This is how people and businesses learn. Explanations of this sort have little in common with excuses. Most important, they are not an attempt to escape consequences. Often people tend to initiate this kind of analysis as a result of experiencing negative consequences.

Sometimes an explanation is helpful in your interpersonal relationships at work. If something you have said or done has made a close colleague angry, you need to analyze the situation in your own mind and later with your colleague to get the relationship back on track.

After You Disagree with a Colleague

To process a disagreement with a colleague, wait until both of you have cooled off. If not, the discussion will probably drift into who was right and who was wrong. There is no better way to destroy a good working relationship.

Keep the focus on how you want the relationship to be in the future rather than on what went wrong in the past. You must, however, understand what went wrong in order to fix it for the future. This takes real sensitivity to the other person's feelings.

If you find the conversation drifting toward who was right, and you can't let the other person be even partly right, it is best to break off the discussion until you have had time to cool down further.

Conducting a "Lessons Learned" Meeting

In analyzing a recent project you may find that your department met some of the project's goals and let others lapse, resulting in a mixed outcome. Because you have already paid the tuition, you might as well learn what went wrong so you don't have to pay the same price again.

When a project goes wrong, the follow-up meeting needs to be closer to a brainstorming session than a cross-examination. It must be clear to everyone that the purpose is not to assign blame or praise but to learn how to prevent similar mistakes in the future.

You, the person in charge, are responsible for setting the tone. If you are filling out evaluation forms while people are talking, they will understand that there are consequences to avoid. You will get excuses instead of analysis. Even if you're only "filling out the forms" in your mind, people will know. Employees can sense evaluation.

They will read it in the way you listen and the kinds of questions you ask. Most important, they will remember what has happened as a result of this kind of meeting in the past.

If people are not being as candid or as analytical as you would like, this is a clear sign that they expect some blame to be assigned as a result of the meeting. If this happens, initiate a discussion about it. The worst thing you can do is pull rank and chew people out for making excuses—then they will be sure they are being evaluated.

The idea of putting yourself in the other person's reality, which we discussed earlier in this chapter, works well here too. You could say, "It seems that you're worried that my reason for being here is to figure out who's to blame for the problems in this project. I get the idea you don't feel it's safe to discuss certain issues."

If people don't pick up on this and start responding less defensively, you have a good indication that they don't trust you or the culture of the company, with you as its representative. In this case, you may need an outside facilitator for a discussion of the trust issue before you can find out what went wrong with the project.

Increased Tension Can Be a Positive Sign

Another element that distinguishes productive explanations from excuses is the level of tension; explanations usually increase tension rather than reducing it. Responsibility increases tension but it improves results.

For example, as a result of your discussions with your colleague, it is likely that you both will come away feeling you have to work harder to maintain the working relationship. You may feel some relief from clearing the air or from realizing that the other person values the relationship as much as you do, but you won't get the total loss of tension that characterizes vindication. (If you do come away feeling vindicated, there are probably still some hard feelings left.)

If the only conclusion from the "lessons learned" session is that you did all the right things and the market is messed up, you would have accomplished as much by going out for a beer together. The most productive result of such a meeting is having people come away with a clearer idea of what they have to do to make things work better the next time around. They may not feel better, but they should have a solid idea of what they have to do to resolve the problems.

The ideal is for everyone to come away knowing how they can work harder and smarter next time. If you sacrifice a scapegoat, many people will feel relieved but no one will learn anything except how to avoid ending up on the altar next time (usually by coming up with more and better excuses).

"We Want Results, Not Excuses!"

Many corporate cultures consider themselves to be results oriented. "We don't accept excuses here. Or explanations. We wants results!" Approaching the issue this way does not do away with excuses. It merely moves them to a different point in the process.

In organizations that see themselves as competitive and results driven, the consequences of making mistakes are usually very high. Excuses in this sort of environment are seldom verbal and after the fact; they would be too late to prevent any consequences. The best excuse in this kind of environment gets you out while the getting is good. An "excuse" here is the one people come up with to bail out of a project that is going bad.

The project is going sour. There are some problems with design, and the market is looking pretty soft. Jack (the Shark in the Brooks Brothers Suit) has been around the block enough times to recognize the signs. This project has a real chance of going down the drain and taking someone's career with it. The loss won't be his, of course; it's time to make his excuses about why he needs a new assignment and to groom someone else to take the fall.

Jack chooses Willis, bright, up-and-coming, and ambitious. Willis will think being placed in charge of the project is a real step forward in his career. His vanity will prevent him from asking, "Why me?" until it's too late and Jack is safely distanced.

Jack promotes Willis and moves out. Willis beams and schmoozes, trying out his newfound authority like a Christmas toy. Meanwhile, the older, more experienced people are excusing themselves from the project quietly—or sometimes noisily. Several of them provoke disagreements with Willis that get them taken out of the game. Later, when the project goes down, they can say, "I told him but he didn't listen. He just got mad and threw me out."

The people with the most experience and skill are bailing out. We know it's a cliché, but the image of rats leaving a sinking ship does suggest itself. These rats might have been able to prevent the ship from sinking. They knew the culture of their company well enough, however, to decide that there were no rewards for working hard and failing. To them, the probability of punishment for failure was much higher than the chances of reward for success. They made their excuses and got out.

When the project inevitably falls apart, they can blame its failure on the inexperienced leadership. After all, it's results that count. People who don't get results have to face the consequences—unless they know enough to get out while the getting is good.

Protecting Yourself from the Bull

What can you do to protect yourself from excuses that don't always work? Remember, they hurt the people who make them and the people who believe them.

Judge yourself on the results of your actions rather than by your intentions. Apply these standards to others as well.

Pay attention to what you're saying to yourself. Excuses work only if you don't pay attention to what you're actually saying.

Evaluate yourself by stepping out of your own reality and seeing yourself as others see you.

If you practice these three steps, you will be safe from the Bull of Excuses and from the other Sacred Bulls we describe.

Chapter Eleven

THE "RIGHT" BULL
There's a Right Way and a Wrong Way—My Way Is Right

S arah is never wrong—that's just all there is to it. If someone suggests that she made a mistake, she will cite rules and regulations, policies and procedures, state and federal law, and even passages from the Bible (she'd use the Koran, too, if it bolstered her argument) that prove that she is right and you are wrong.

She will point out, loudly and in great detail, that she did exactly what she was supposed to, but other people somehow messed up, misunderstood, or at the very least did not give her the information she needed.

The most difficult admission in any language is "I was wrong." Many of us regard being wrong as so unthinkable that we are willing to make fools of ourselves to avoid it. This Sacred Bull says you must fight to be right, demand to be right—even make a fool of yourself to be right—because the only alternative is to be wrong.

The "Right" Bull will try to convince you that if you

know you're right, it doesn't matter what other people think. If they disagree, it's their problem. Being right means you never have to say you're sorry—or thank-you, either.

Being right feels good inside, but it is seldom worth the cost. Being right is not an absolute state ordained by laws of nature. It is a prize for which other people will also compete. Being right is a privilege you can demand if you're powerful enough. Or it is a favor other people do for you by consenting to be wrong. (If you don't repay them by agreeing to be wrong yourself, they may resent you.) Being right doesn't exist by itself in a vacuum. If you are right, somebody else has to be wrong.

This Bull Can't Even See Gray

It always seems that Sarah is the only person in the office who never makes a mistake. People cringe when they have to deal with her. She hears criticism even in the most innocent comments and always feels compelled to defend herself against it—to the death. The more she senses an attack, the more defensive she will be. People can't talk to her about their problems because they know what will happen. Sarah will declare, in injured tones, "You're the one with the problem!"

Surely Sarah must know that the defensive spectacle she makes of herself when she is criticized is far more damaging to her credibility and relationships with other people than almost any mistake she might be accused of making. Yet she persists in arguing each point as if her whole value as a person were in the balance. Sarah believes it is.

It is unfortunate that the words *right* and *wrong* mean

both "correct" and "incorrect" and "good" and "evil." The "Right" Bull will tell you that any question of right and wrong is really a question of good and evil. Sarah wants to feel she is competent, conscientious, and valuable as an employee. If she is wrong, she feels accused of being incompetent, lazy, and inferior.

Sarah sees criticism as an accusation that she must answer if she is to continue to think of herself as a good person. To be good she has to be right.

The "Right" Bull will try to convince you that right and wrong are absolutes and that it is always possible and necessary to know which is which. Not only can't this Bull see colors, he can't even see gray. To the "Right" Bull everything is either white or black. Like his cousin, the Bull of Blame, with which he works closely, the "Right" Bull provides overly simple answers to complex or ambiguous questions. If you think that following this Bull will make your life miserable, you're absolutely right.

BE RIGHT OR BE EFFECTIVE

Often the world offers a choice between being right and being effective. For you to be right, somebody else has to be wrong. The result can put major dents in your effectiveness.

Sarah's coworkers can't stand her. She has locked horns with most of them over minor issues, about which, of course, she was right and everybody else was wrong. Instead of getting the respect and acknowledgment she so desperately wants, she has an office full of people who owe her one, or who avoid her, or who make fun of her behind her back. She begins to feel that there is more to defend against—and she's right about that, too.

Sarah sees the situation only as defending herself against accusations of being wrong. She cannot see that other people view her defenses as attacks against them. There's a Bull standing in her way, saying, "There's a right way and a wrong way, and your way is right. Just explain it and they'll understand."

Rick, Sarah's boss, would rather get audited by the IRS than sit through another of her self-righteous speeches. If he implies the slightest criticism of Sarah's work, he knows he can expect at least a half hour of explanation. Today he made the mistake of asking where was the report he had assigned her last week. His ears are still ringing from Sarah's lecture.

"Well, knowing what I know and considering the support I got, I did exactly what any intelligent, reasonable person would have done," she began heatedly. "The problem was that nobody thought to tell me that the report had to be finished today. I was told that other priorities were higher on the list."

With an injured glare, she added, "Besides that, the figures I got were incomplete. And my software doesn't handle the data the way you asked for it. Also, did you know that three of my staff are out sick? And, really, what does everybody expect when my department is the most overloaded in the entire division and. . . ."

Midway through the harangue, Rick stopped listening and his thoughts turned sarcastic. How had he managed to hire the only beacon of right and reason in a universe of chaos and error? How had he gotten so lucky? All he had wanted to know was when the report would be ready.

All of Sarah's excuses are the kind that lower tension for her by raising it for other people—especially for Rick, her boss. Sarah believes Rick has it in for her and, again, she's absolutely right.

Rick hates what Sarah brings out in him. He doesn't think such cynical thoughts are appropriate or productive for a manager. But just asking her a simple question can lead to Sarah's saying what Rick hears as "If you were doing your job as a manager, I'd have no trouble getting everything done correctly and on time."

"You Take Things Too Personally"

Rick would like to feel like a good person, too, but it's very difficult around Sarah. Even though she is talented and good at her job, he would love to get rid of her. Of course, he knows you can't fire someone for being obnoxious. Besides, he doesn't believe in that kind of power abuse. On the other hand, Sarah is a disruption not only to him but to the whole department. People are always complaining to him about her. Many times he has tried to approach Sarah about her behavior. He tells her she takes things too personally, but she just doesn't listen.

Rick has run square into one of the major problems with defensive people. It is very difficult to talk to them about what they're doing. Most of the things he can think of to say about this kind of behavior—"You're being defensive," "You can't take criticism"—he knows in advance will be taken as attacks.

Rick falls back on the phrase most people use, "You take things too personally." (From his point of view, this is the most supportive way he can say what he wants Sarah to understand.) He is correct, of course, but it won't do any good. This is another of the million examples life offers every day that being correct carries no guarantees that you'll be effective.

From Sarah's point of view, it *is* personal when people say she's wrong. Telling her she takes things too personally becomes just another attack, and a confusing one.

She takes the statement too personally to understand it. What she hears them saying is that she is bad. She then feels compelled to defend herself with explanations that feel like attacks.

When Sarah asks, "What do you mean?" she leaves Rick right where he started. He is still fumbling for the right words to say, words that Sarah can hear and that will help her handle criticism a little better.

IF YOU TAKE THINGS TOO PERSONALLY

For the record, if anyone has ever told you, "You take things too personally," they probably were unable to clarify what they meant. We bet they meant you have a hard time handling criticism. If someone suggests that you made a mistake, it's possible that you act as if they said you were a bad person. Your defense in such a situation is usually perceived as an attack.

When life offers you a choice between being right and being effective, you choose to be right. This Sacred Bull is telling you there is an absolute right and wrong in the situation, and you are the one who's right. What the Bull doesn't tell you is that this makes other people wrong and that they will feel compelled (goaded by the same Bull) to fight you.

As Grandfather used to say, "If one person calls you a horse, you can laugh about it. If two people call you a horse, think about it. If three people call you a horse, buy a saddle." If at least two people have suggested that you and Sarah are riding the same Bull, they are probably saying that you take things too personally as a nice way of saying you can't handle criticism. Resist the impulse to skip the rest of this chapter, take a deep breath, and hang on to your saddle horn.

Criticism may save you. Every criticism has two parts: attack and information. You are probably great at picking up the attack part, but you may be missing out on the information. That information may be vital. Criticism may save you money or save your career.

Studies show that defensive people get passed over for promotion. (If you're the boss and don't need a promotion, you might consider the studies that suggest that bosses who can't take criticism have worse bottom lines because people don't tell them what they need to know.)

People who have a hard time with criticism are often perfectionists. They think they should do everything right, and they work very hard to make things right. Other people don't realize how much perfectionists criticize themselves, so when someone else makes a critical comment, it really hurts.

Wait to respond. You can learn to use a simple trick that may be helpful in handling criticism: When people make a critical comment about you, hold your response for two days. Don't say anything. During that time try to think about what they said. Ask yourself, "If the criticism were true, what would I do? How would I feel? What information is here that I can use?"

For example, if someone said, "You sure can't take criticism," what could you say? You could say, "If that were true, I would make a big deal of it when people say I'm wrong. I'd try to explain why it wasn't my fault. I'd probably point out the things *they* were doing wrong."

Recognize that people may be reacting to you as they typically react to defensive people. They avoid telling you certain things because they think you will make such a big deal out of them. That's the part that can cost you.

Ask what you can do. When you have tried on the criticism for two days, go back to the person and ask what you can do to make it easier to talk to you. Then try *that* on for size.

The trick is never to answer a criticism with a criticism or an excuse that lowers tension for you by raising it for the person talking to you. Instead, respond only with thinking and action. It gets the "Right" Bull every time.

The Way out of the Trap of Defensiveness

Most people, even the most defensive, don't believe other people criticize them purposely to hurt them. They just get lost in the hurt feelings and hop onto the "Right" Bull. The rest is history waiting to be written.

People who can't take criticism tend to see every situation as having a right and a wrong side that can be decided through discussion and argument. To prove they are right, they fall into the trap of defensiveness. A way out of this trap is to ask, "Are we both acting in good faith?" rather than, "Who is right and who is wrong here?"

If you stop yourself and ask, "Is the other person acting in good faith?" you may be able to short-circuit the automatic process of defensiveness. You may be able to recognize that the other person, like you, is doing the best she can. This may open a door through which you can begin to see the other person's point of view. You may have to drag yourself, kicking and screaming, through this door, but it will be worth it.

Often, as soon as the other person realizes that you can see what she's talking about, the attack can cease and negotiation can begin. If you negotiate, it's possible you may both get what you want. You can't, however, negotiate over who's right and who's wrong. Despite what any Bull tells you, there are no prizes for being right.

This Bull Stands on Principle

Principles can often be the pastures wherein Sacred Bulls may safely graze (the sheep had better watch out). People's principles can dictate what they consider the right kind of action in a situation. It has always amazed us how convenient principles can be for the people who hold them and how inconvenient they can be for everyone else.

To Judith, nursing supervisor for several units of a large hospital, following regulations is more than a way to protect the hospital from lawsuits, it is a matter of moral principle.

To Judith, the nursing procedures for each of her units were handed down from Mount Sinai—where she did her training. They are the right procedures and the ones everyone must follow. There is a way to enter chart notes. There is a way to take blood pressure. There is a way to give meds. There is even a particular way to answer the phone. If anyone deviates from any of the procedures, Judith considers it her duty to browbeat the offender into submission.

Today she called Melissa, a young nurse, on the carpet.

Judith's metallic voice clanged across the nurses' station. "You must always realize that your patients' lives are in your hands. Because you didn't follow the correct procedures, lives were placed in jeopardy."

Melissa's eyes widened in alarm. Judith's eyes narrowed. "Perhaps it is because you don't have what it takes to be a nurse. Maybe you ought to consider another, less-responsible career that will tolerate the kind of lazy, self-indulgent behavior that seems to be the only thing of which you are capable. Do I make myself clear?"

"Yes, ma'am," Melissa whispered as she slunk back to her post.

Judith wheeled and marched down the corridor. Perhaps that dangerously incompetent twit would think twice before she failed again in her duty to answer the floor telephone within the requisite five rings.

Being a good nurse is obviously a moral issue with Judith. She is totally blind to the idea that sadistically abusing an employee for a minor infraction may also have moral implications.

Simon doesn't believe in being soft on employees. It's a matter of principle with him. His people need to respect his authority. Being employed, after all, is a privilege. Employees should demonstrate their worthiness by showing a willingness to put the company's welfare ahead of their own (read that "do exactly what Simon tells them without talking back").

Simon considers it a matter of principle to make life difficult for any employees who have a problem with that.

Rico has his principles, too. As a skilled technician he knows how the job should be done, who should do it, and how long it should take to get it done. No manager who lacks Rico's experience and credentials can presume to dictate what he or his department should have to do.

Rico's principle, stated simply, is "Nobody gets to tell me what to do."

Carol thinks her work should stand on its own. It is against her principles to blow her own horn. Anybody who cared to check could see the wonderful job she's doing for the company. Her skills, her contributions to the team, her value to the organization should be obvious. It should be equally obvious that she deserves a raise.

To Carol, it is a matter of major ingratitude that, except for minuscule cost-of-living raises, she has remained at the same salary level for eight years.

It is a matter of principle to her that somebody should try to do something about that—anybody but Carol herself.

Sacred Bulls often dictate people's principles. Being right means you can push people around or feel pushed around and resentful. Being right also means you never have to say you're sorry.

The "Right" Bull is always ready to lend a hand to his cousins. He is particularly helpful to the Bull of Shortcuts and Blind Spots in convincing you that the right way to do things is always the way that is easiest and most comfortable for you.

The "Right" Bull is also quite friendly to the Bull of Denial by helping him to conceal authority issues, power trips, and passive-aggressive tendencies. None of this applies to people who are doing things the right way, does it? (Right.)

A Manager Who Knows THE Way to Be Right

Some well-meaning managers know the job so well that they think there is only one way to do it. They assume their way is the only way, so they feel justified in micromanaging. They don't realize they can end up wasting money and talent.

Bart was the company's top sales rep for eight years running, then was promoted to sales manager. If there's one thing Bart knows, it's how to sell products. From his many years of successful sales experience, he has ideas about everything it takes to make it big in sales.

He knows what kind of suit you should wear and what kind of briefcase you should carry. He knows what kind of attitude a successful sales rep should have. Complaining about anything is a sign of poor motivation. A messy desk is a sign of a cluttered mind.

Bart doesn't even like people to write with pencils because he thinks having an eraser encourages sloppy think-

ing. He always says that people who write with a pen are more apt to get it right the first time.

He has developed sales scripts for all categories of products. He encourages rehearsal, with monitoring by the reps' supervisors, to make sure people don't deviate from the script.

What Bart expects is 110 percent commitment. What he gets is resentment and poor performance from people who used to have very good sales records before Bart took over. They just don't want to be Bart Clones.

Bart may know a lot about sales, but his knowledge makes him less effective as a manager. He believes that what he knows is *the* way to do it right rather than one way to do it right. There isn't a manager alive who believes micromanagement works, yet many managers practice it. When people say they don't believe in something but do it anyway, you know there must be a Sacred Bull standing in the way, blocking the view.

SOMETHING'S GOTTA GIVE

Other people may be just as convinced as you are that their opinion is the right one. When an irresistible force meets an immovable object, something's gotta give.

Tula is one of the more talented sales reps who works for Bart. She resents his micromanaging style and doesn't care who knows it. She has an MBA in Sales and Marketing and can cite studies that show that overcontrol hurts performance. She made a presentation on sales management for Bart. She made charts, reviewed studies, and even gave him books to read.

Her theme was, essentially, "Micromanagement sucks," but the point was lost on Bart. He agrees that micromanage-

ment is ineffective but does not see that that's what he is doing. What he does see is that Tula probably has some authority and motivation issues that he needs to do something about.

Both Bart and Tula are right, but being right won't do either of them much good. Tula believes Bart's micromanaging shows that he is not qualified to run the department. She is angry and contemptuous, and stops just short of insubordination. Nevertheless, Bart shouldn't be doing things this way. Tula's right.

Bart thinks Tula is a center for discontent in his department. Her problems with his management style and the way she handles them means she doesn't belong in his department. He's right also.

Something's gotta give. In the corporate world, when two people disagree and they're both right, the one with the most power is more right. The pink slip goes to Tula, unjustly perhaps and wastefully. She was one of Bart's better people. Let's say she got trampled by the "Right" Bull.

How to Work for a Micromanager

Don't let Tula's Bull run over you as well. If you work for a micromanaging boss, immediately weed that word *micromanager* out of your vocabulary. Call it something less provocative. Don't set up a situation in which your boss has to be wrong for you to get a little latitude in decision making.

Just because your boss should be managing differently doesn't mean he will if only you point it out. Negotiation, not accusation, is what's called for here. The idea of product versus process can also be helpful. Here are some tips.

Ask a lot of questions about the desired product. What does your boss expect from you: a certain amount of sales, a report that will present certain information or look good to the people upstairs? Ask for specifics.

Find out the criteria for an acceptable product. What would it look like? What would it do? Who would approve of it? What would its effects be?

Negotiate so that providing the product becomes part of the responsibilities of your job. Most micromanagers are not so obsessed with process that they prefer it to results. Your chances for latitude improve if you say, "What you want is a product that meets the following criteria by [a specified date]. I will take responsibility for providing that product."

This approach will negotiate control of the process. It also can point out, more gently than an accusation, that there is no clear product specified or the only criteria for success is doing it the boss's way. If your boss still balks, you can say cheerfully, "Okay then, you tell me what to do and I'll do it!" If it's possible for a micromanager to take a hint, he or she will pick up on this one.

You may choose to continue pressing for certain areas of authority. Try to set things up so that both of you can be right. Remember Tula—and review chapter 9 on fairness.

When Being Right Makes You Ineffective

Among the less-talented sales reps on his team, Bart's micromanagement style is creating people who can't think for themselves and who have little reason to try. His top sales people resent him so much that they are trying to transfer out of his department. Meanwhile, they will fight him all the way. Bart is limiting his department to whatever he is capable of. No one generates new ideas, which is fine with Bart because his ideas are the only right ones anyway.

Sometimes being right can make a manager ineffective. Bart knows what it takes for him to do his best. He has done a lot of thinking about it. If he follows a particular procedure, then the sales come in. He believes it is the procedure, not the person, that does the selling.

Like most micromanagers, Bart controls the *process*—how people do what they do—in the belief that if you control the process the product will take care of itself. This would probably be true if there were only one correct process. It is an easy error to make, especially by managers who are very experienced with the technical aspects of the job but are not very experienced with people.

Bart gains control at the expense of independent thinking. Aside from the resentment and retaliation that micromanagement breeds, it also doesn't work because no manager can be everywhere or do it all.

Here's a good test to see if you are letting the "Right" Bull lead you into micromanagement: Think in terms of *product*—what you want people to accomplish—and *process*—how they get there. Your thoughts about product should be specific, detailed, clear, and lengthy. If you're a manager, your job is to specify the product. *Let the employees develop the process themselves.* No amount of controlling the process will assure you of a good product, especially if you aren't clear about what product you want.

It is much easier to manage the process. (The Bull that says, "What I don't like isn't important," will try to tell you that if you manage the process the product will take care of itself. This is bull manure—but *Sacred* Bull manure.)

Look at your own management style. If you are devoting more than about 20 percent of your time to managing process, you may be micromanaging. If you want people to take responsibility for their jobs, they have to have control of the process. If they don't have control of that, what else is left? Responsibility for their mistakes. And believe us, there will be mistakes.

WHEN THE BOSS IS RIGHT

Some managers who seem obsessed with having things done their way are actually very bright, competent people with good judgment and reasoning skills. They excel at anticipating difficulties and planning for them. They desperately want their employees to be as capable as they are. The problem is that their own competence often stands in the way.

Everybody at the magazine knows Arthur is brilliant. No one else knows the field the way he does. His depth and breadth of knowledge intimidates even the senior editors. So does his personality—he does not tolerate sloppy thinking. At all. If you haven't done your research on an article or your reasoning is not all it should be, Arthur will attack you publicly and without mercy.

Arthur is great at bringing out the best in the top 1 percent of new editors. They are the ones who recognize that Arthur's style of thinking is the most important skill he has to teach. To learn it, they must be willing to be his personal apprentices. They have to hang on his every word to figure out what he is saying, tolerate a half-dozen rewrites of each article, and accept heaps of humiliation. After about a year of feeling stupid, they realize they have learned something that will shape the rest of their careers.

Arthur is a master at his job. If you want to learn from him, you have to become his apprentice. This means accepting a subordinate (and perhaps somewhat degrading) position and being able to figure out what he's trying to teach you without being told specifically.

What people like Arthur try to teach is usually a matter of style and perception rather than specific behaviors. One of the best ways to learn those fine discriminations is to watch someone who is very good at making them and try to see what that person sees.

No matter how valuable this experience is to the company and the field, however, it is not management.

Arthur is matchless at developing highly talented and confident people. Unfortunately, that is not his only responsibility. He has twenty-six other editors in his department. Most of them want a manager, not a Zen master. He tries to instruct them in how to think about words and their power, but his lessons are beyond them. Every day at lunch they trade stories about the Czar on the Eighth Floor. Arthur doesn't care. They are beneath his notice.

As brilliant as he is, Arthur is not doing very well the job he is paid to do. Any of us could do great things with the one or two top people we have to manage. A manager, however, is responsible for all of the people in the department. You have to know how to change your approach to get through to the most people. If you have only one style of dealing with people—even if it's the right one—you will create a lot of mistakes. Usually the people you manage will be the ones who are making them.

There are other problems, too. When it comes to specific management decisions, sometimes Arthur is too right for his own good. Consider, for example, his insistence on proper grammar. Arthur will not allow his writers to use colloquial English: no informal references, no conversational tone and, God forbid, no slang. The result is a maga-

zine stylistically reminiscent of Jane Austen, albeit (as Arthur might put it) lacking that estimable woman's sly wit.

The magazine has become stilted and out of touch, losing the younger market to hip, new publications that are attracting big readerships and bigger ad campaigns. The people upstairs have been telling Arthur that his lofty standards are costing them money and resources.

Arthur is profoundly cynical about the quality of journalism, especially as performed by the young editors in his department, and about management's insistence on a good bottom line. In the old days, when his profession was not so finance driven, he might have been kept in a position of power. The only way to have power at his magazine is to be a manager.

Arthur knows that he's in decline. His position is in jeopardy and his results do not match his brilliance. Were it not a cliché, he would say his days are numbered. His cynicism and crankiness are increasing exponentially.

Arthur's Choice

Arthur has to make the choice between being right and being effective. The first thing he must decide is whether he wants to be a manager. In many companies this is the only option available for a talented senior person. (In some ways this is like using a Maserati to haul a trailer.) The ideal solution would be for upper management to find Arthur a position more congruent with his skills and talents, one that does not involve a demotion or emeritus (read that "out to pasture") status.

If Arthur chooses to be a manager, he needs to hitch up. That means paying attention to and taking responsibility for demographics, dollars, and B+ editors, all of which he has considered beneath him. He may be right about this, but being right gets him nothing but pain, cynicism, and a feeling of failure. He must realize that there is more than one way to train a fledgling editor. He can learn ways to counteract the effects of the Sacred Bull that intones, "There's a right way and a wrong way; my way is right."

His job is teaching. Seeing his job as *teaching* can help Arthur recognize that people quickly become resentful and burned out if all they hear is criticism. He needs to consider how to get his ideas across in ways that his staff can understand and achieve, rather than unconsciously using his own life as an example for other people to follow.

He must be relevant. He also must stop believing that being right absolves him from any responsibility for being relevant. Because Arthur believes his method is right, he presents information without regard for what his young editors consider important, possible, or even interesting.

The editors nod politely, agree with him, and tune him out because they can't understand him. (Most people have had years of training in looking as if they're listening when they actually aren't. This is one of the most valuable skills they learn in school.)

He must be clear. As a manager it is Arthur's responsibility to see that people understand him. To understand, they will have to listen. He will need to let them know immediately that there is something in it for them, besides incomprehensible lectures and verbal abuse, if they listen to what he has to teach. This will be especially important whenever he has to teach them something they don't want to hear. It is Arthur's job to make what he has to say clear and accessible. Being right does not guarantee being understood.

THE RIGHT KIND OF MANAGER

Marissa and Weston are middle managers in the same company. Both believe in team playing, but one plays on the employee team and the other on the management team.

Marissa sees herself, first and foremost, as the protector of her team, the person who makes it possible for them to do their jobs with the least possible difficulty and interference. She makes sure they have what they need and tries to insulate them from what she calls the "political bull" that comes down from above. She often finds herself fighting upper management to make sure her team is treated fairly.

She hates meetings, committees, and blue-ribbon panels. None of those experimental demonstration programs for her, either. She prefers doing what she calls "real work."

Marissa is usually available in her department to listen to her employees. Sometimes she even changes her mind based on what they say. They think she's tough but fair. She expects a day and a half's work for a day's pay. She knows what people are doing and how they're doing. If you step out of line, you'll hear about it. Marissa doesn't praise easily, but when she does it means a lot. Her employees would walk on water for her.

Marissa's department is tops in overall productivity. Her costs are not the lowest but her error rate is near zero, and turnover is practically nonexistent. (Well, she did lose a person a few years ago when an employee got married and moved to Nebraska. People lined up to apply for the vacant spot, and it was quickly filled. There were lots of transfer requests; there always are. Everybody wants to work for Marissa.)

Weston, the other manager, sees himself as a starter on the management team. He takes the business of running a company very seriously. He's always on committees and panels and is involved in the latest management training and experimental programs. He spends a lot of time away from his department in meetings, planning sessions, and general bull sessions with other managers. He's great at networking and is always among the first to know what's up.

Whenever the company introduces new equipment or new procedures, Weston's department is the first to try them out. He sees this as giving his people an edge. His employees see it as making their jobs confusing and unpredictable.

Weston practices what he considers a hands-off management style. "If you have good people, and I do," he always says, "they don't need constant direction."

Most of his departmental communication is through daily meetings with his two lead people. Every morning he gets a five-minute review of what's going on in the department and gives his directions for the day. If there are problems, his leads always know where they can find him. Weston's employees, however, would like a little more of his time and energy. One departmental clown recently rigged up a milk carton with his picture on it above the caption, "Have you seen this man?" Weston was not amused.

His department numbers look good. Productivity and errors are moderate, but he achieves a good bottom line with relentless cost controls. Weston is never afraid to cut hours or do whatever is necessary to keep costs in line. He even uses turnover to his advantage by keeping positions open as long as possible.

Weston relates best with management. His team doesn't. They feel they hardly know him. He's not unfair; he's just one of "them"—another manager.

Marissa and Weston are managers with very different styles. People want to work for Marissa, but in most companies management wants people like Weston working for them. (Rewards and promotions seldom come for doing good work with those below; they come for having good relationships with those above.)

Which manager's approach is right? Both are right, depending on the way you look at them. Both can be wrong as well, if doing things the way they do doesn't get them the results they want. It is the *results* that are important. Try to stop thinking in terms of right or wrong management. Instead, think of correct and incorrect management based on the approaches that produce the results you're looking for.

Protecting Yourself from the "Right" Bull

How do you protect yourself from the "Right" Bull? The answer is absurdly simple. *Let other people be right.* Recognize that being right is a costly privilege rather than an absolute state of grace. Of course this does not mean that you should always give in. Instead, work with a situation in your mind until you can see it in a way in which *both* of you can be right at the same time.

When you can do that, you're coming closer than any Sacred Bull can lead you to seeing the world as it really is. For example, in the case of Marissa and Weston, there is no right way to manage. There are tradeoffs and compromises each can make. Each can learn from the other's approach.

From the Psych Lab to You

Being right seems so important, but what does being right really mean? How do we know we're right?

Psychology has been studying human behavior in an organized way for more than 150 years. We don't have all the answers, but we have discovered certain effects and rules that seem to show up no matter what the setting—the psychological laboratory, the family, the classroom, and on the job. It helps to think of these rules as the Laws of Gravity of Human Behavior: People follow them whether they know about them or not.

People misuse and misunderstand these rules every day in many businesses. Instead they follow Sacred Bulls. By knowing about these rules and how they work, you can organize the way you do your job so that these rules start working for you instead of against you.

Immediacy

People go after immediate gratification. They will do whatever has the most immediate benefits. This is why most people feel such pressure to work fast and sloppily. The immediate reward—finishing the task—is usually much more powerful than a reward that may never come for doing it well.

This principle explains why the Bull of Denial and the Bull of Shortcuts and Blind Spots have such power. They cause us to trade long-term success for long-term comfort. It's a classic bad deal, but it sure feels good when they offer it.

Response Hierarchy

People return to old habits under stress. When the pressure is on, you are most likely to do what you know best. Anyone can do things differently under ideal conditions. Under stress, however, you forget, then go back to "the way you've always done it," whether it's right or not. You will also convince yourself (the Bull of Denial helps convince you) that the old way is the new way.

Just telling people what you want them to do is not

enough. To turn new ways of thinking and acting into habits, you will need repeated practice. (Psychologists call this *overlearning*.)

Many of the ideas and new ways of doing things may sound interesting and practical as you read them. They are, but they will take some effort and trial and error to integrate into your daily life. Habits are hard to change, especially when the "Right" Bull convinces you that they aren't habits at all but the way things are supposed to be done. Don't be discouraged. (Whatever you do, don't try to follow our advice perfectly!)

Comfort Zone

A little anxiety improves performance, but a lot of anxiety destroys it. An inner circle of thoughts and actions is the "comfort zone" in which you usually operate. In the circle outside it, the Circle of Challenge, performance improves and life is enhanced.

To be psychologically healthy, you have to do things that are new, different, more difficult, or a little scary. If you listen to the Bull of Shortcuts and Blind Spots, you'll stay in your comfort zone. Not only will you keep making the same old mistakes, but your life will seem dull and uninteresting.

The Circle of Challenge has definite boundaries. When the pressure goes up beyond a certain point, performance drops drastically. Few people operate well in a panic. They either freeze or just go back to their old habits.

The Bull of Self-Interest misinterprets this rule, however. He believes that the farther people are forced out of their comfort zone, the more their performance improves. This Bull will suggest strategies that inhibit performance in the name of improving it, such as threatening people with losing their jobs. The Bull prevents these managers from seeing that people who are insecure about their jobs are less productive and more concerned with covering their own posteriors.

The Bull of Denial can prevent you from seeing the sadistic pleasure power trips like this can bring you. If you don't see it, it isn't there. Right?

Positive Reinforcement

Rewarding positive behavior works better than punishing negative behavior. This is the rule the "Right" Bull helps you forget. The best way to change the way people act is to catch them being good and reward them. The problem is that it feels so much better and is so much easier to punish them for making mistakes. The Bull of Blame will love you for it. Learning to use praise rather than punishment takes a lot of practice. It just doesn't feel "right."

Halo Effect

What you see is not always what you get. We see what we expect to see. People who look good and seem to think and act the way we do are considered smarter, more creative, and nicer than people who are different. This effect is so strong that first impressions often control all our subsequent interactions with other people.

We have to be very careful not to base our whole opinion of the people around us on how attractive they are or how much they agree with us. We always give preference to people who follow the *same* Sacred Bulls as we do.

A word to the wise about business success: If you don't make a good first impression (or if your Sacred Bulls cause you to alienate people), you are not likely to be given a second chance. This is not because employers are mean or unfair. It is just that once they have a perception of you, it is very hard to change.

Self-Fulfilling Prophecy

Within limits, what people think will happen to them is what happens. We all unconsciously make choices that lead us to the future we expect. If you believe you can do something, or if you think you can't you will usually be right. This principle explains why motivation is considered so important in business (and why motivational seminars are such big business).

Internal motivation and belief are powerful stimuli, but they are not very accessible from the outside. People's internal beliefs are a product of years of experience. They don't change for long because of a lecture or a pep talk or a sermon. We just *think* they do because of the Hawthorne Effect.

Hawthorne Effect

Whatever you do to improve performance will improve it for about two weeks. This is one of the first principles discovered by industrial psychologists, and it's been confusing people ever since. You have probably observed the Hawthorne effect at work: For a few days after a training seminar, everybody's performance improves. Two weeks later, it's business as usual.

Remember, to determine whether something is actually working the way you want it to, you have to keep teaching and rewarding the new behavior and measure it a month or more later.

In dealing with yourself or the people you work with, training seminars, new programs—even books by experts—may be helpful but they cannot substitute for setting clear priorities, checking on a regular basis, offering immediate rewards for positive behavior, and giving information about performance. Nothing beats that. Nothing can, because it's the way we're wired. If anybody tells you there's another way to do it, they're just handing you a bunch of Sacred Bull.

PROTECTING YOURSELF FROM SACRED BULLS

The point of this book has been to challenge seldom-examined beliefs that hold you back at work. Throughout, we have asked you to look at your own thoughts and behaviors more critically than usual. It takes courage to think about yourself in this way. We hope we have given you some opportunity to be courageous—even if it wasn't easy.

We have seen the damage Sacred Bulls can do, not only in the day-to-day situations we have chronicled in each chapter but also in deeper, more significant areas. We hope this book can help you avoid the destructive effects of these creatures.

Doing psychotherapy every day provides many examples of people wrapped up in distress of their own devising. There is a fierce joy in seeing them fight their way out and sharing their exhilaration when they begin to realize "I don't have to do this any more." It is the fighting that makes the freedom so sweet.

The fight has to be directed. It is so easy to become

confused and to see the people you work with and live with (rather than your own beliefs) as the enemy. That is why we gave you Sacred Bulls. If you want to improve your feelings about your job and your life, fight with *them*, not with the people around you.

You don't win this fight by snorting and bellowing—leave that to the Bulls—but by paying attention to yourself and to the implications of your thoughts and actions. Most people are starving for this kind of attention. The Bull of Denial who says, "I don't see it so it isn't there," keeps them from paying serious attention to themselves.

If you keep paying attention, you win. The prizes are simple but valuable. A job worth doing. A life worth living. Feeling successful, even happy.

What it takes for people to feel good about themselves and to be psychologically healthy are just the things Sacred Bulls take away.

A Feeling of Challenge and Accomplishment

To feel good about your job and yourself, you have to feel you're doing something that is worth doing.

The Bull of Blind Spots and Shortcuts who says, "What I don't like can't be important," and the "Nice" Bull who says, "Avoid conflict at all cost," can subtly steer you away from doing the things that are hard for you. These are the very things, however, that can give you the feelings of challenge and accomplishment that make your actions mean something. What is easy and safe never really satisfies.

To protect yourself from these Bulls when you are having a problem, visualize yourself standing at a crossroads. One road is easy; the other is hard. Take the hard one. Sacred Bulls will never follow you down that path. The feelings of challenge and achievement come from taking on what is personally difficult and giving it your best. Especially when you're scared.

A Feeling of Control over Your Life

All Sacred Bulls work by hiding choices from you. They convince you that there is only one way to handle a situation, that other people are in control and there's nothing you can do. Sacred Bulls can make you feel trapped, bogged down, and resentful.

True, there are lots of things that happen in your job that aren't under your control. In that respect all our jobs (and our lives) are like a poker game. You can't control the cards you're dealt, but it's up to you how you play your hand.

The Bull of Blame who says, "It has to be somebody's fault," can cheat you out of your feeling of control over your own life, leaving only your bitterness to hold onto.

To protect yourself from this dangerous beast, you must understand the game and stay aware of your options. Keep asking yourself, "What do I want to happen, and what is the best way to make it happen?" Think of the goal rather than the people standing in the way. The Bull of Blame hates that.

A Feeling of Connection and Trust

If you can't trust other people, you're all alone. Despite what the Bull of Self-Interest says, looking out for Number One does not lead to success and happiness but to alienation and loneliness.

The Bull of Mind Reading who says, "People should know without being told," and the Bull of Perfection who says, "If it's not perfect, it's nothing," will try to convince you to protect yourself by setting your standards so high that no one can measure up. If you don't trust anybody, no one can let you down.

The Bull of Fairness who says, "I don't need to negotiate for what I want; I just want fairness," will convince you that nobody is willing to give you what you deserve. This creature also might talk you into doing unto others before they do unto you.

The "Right" Bull who says, "There's a right way and a wrong way; my way is right," can blind you to the value in other people's perceptions.

These Bulls will make you believe you're in it by yourself and that no one else is worthy enough or safe enough to trust.

You can't do your job in a world full of potential enemies. You'll spend too much time worrying and fighting.

To protect yourself from these devious animals you have to put yourself (kicking and screaming, if need be) into the other person's shoes. There is nothing these Bulls can do that a little empathy won't cure. But with Bulls bellowing in your brain, empathy is the last thing you're likely to think about.

Now that you know about the Sacred Bulls in your life, see the damage they can do, and know what will protect you, we have an important question.

What are you going to do about them?

The Bull of Excuses will tell you there are good reasons why this stuff doesn't apply to you or doesn't mean that you actually have to do anything differently.

We dearly hope no one can hand you *that* kind of Bull any more.

INDEX

ABOUT THE AUTHORS

Albert J. Bernstein, Ph.D., and Sydney Craft Rozen are the authors of the best-selling *DINOSAUR BRAINS: Dealing with All Those Impossible People at Work* and *NEANDERTHALS AT WORK: How People and Politics Can Drive You Crazy and What You Can Do About Them*.

Albert J. Bernstein, Ph.D., is a clinical psychologist in private practice and a business consultant who has worked with a wide variety of corporations and organizations. Dr. Bernstein also writes regularly published business columns, including "Life at Work" in the *Vancouver (Wash.) Columbian*. He lives with his wife Luahna and their children, Jessica and Joshua, in Portland, Oregon.

Sydney Craft Rozen is a writer and editor and has taught college journalism and English. She contributed to *Taming the Dragon in Your Child* by Meg Eastman, Ph.D., and several other best-selling books. She lives with her husband Lee and children, Geoffrey and Amanda, in the Seattle, Washington, area.